THE ESSENTIAL PAR

John Carey is Emeritus Professor at Ox... include studies of John Donne, Charles Dickens and William Makepeace Thackeray, as well as *The Intellectuals and the Masses*, *What Good Are the Arts?* and a life of William Golding. His memoir, *The Unexpected Professor*, was a *Sunday Times* bestseller.

Further praise for *The Essential Paradise Lost*:

'Carey tells us Milton's "is not a static art, but mobile, and constantly readjusting" – an apt characterisation of Carey's craft. Fifty years of intense labour lie behind these rich investigations, making *The Essential Paradise Lost* essential reading.' Willy Maley, *Times Higher Education Supplement*

'An attractive and highly readable *Paradise Lost* . . . Carey's new edition will lead even more readers to its splendours, to wonder at its tragic action, epic music and transcendent strangeness.' Andrew Fuhrmann, *Sydney Review of Books*

'Reader-friendly . . . Carey neatly condenses the argument rather than just cherry-picking an assortment of golden goals from the untiring dazzle and swagger of its verse.' Boyd Tonkin, *Spectator*

JOHN CAREY

THE ESSENTIAL

PARADISE LOST

FABER & FABER

First published in 2017
By Faber & Faber Ltd
Bloomsbury House
74–77 Great Russell Street
London WC1B 3DA
This paperback edition published in 2019

Typeset by Faber & Faber Ltd
Printed and bound by CPI Group (UK) Ltd, Croydon CR0 4YY

A CIP record for this book
is available from the British Library

ISBN 978–0–571–35502–0

2 4 6 8 10 9 7 5 3 1

For Gill

CONTENTS

INTRODUCTION

Why Shorten *Paradise Lost*?

For two and a half centuries after its publication in 1667 *Paradise Lost* was celebrated throughout Europe as a sublime masterpiece, among the greatest achievements of the human intellect. Voltaire, writing in 1727, judged that the poem showed 'something above the reach of human powers'. Now almost no one reads it.

Not to have read it at all – any of it – seems to me a deprivation on a level with – what? Never having listened to a Beethoven symphony? Never having seen a Shakespearean tragedy? Never having been to a religious service? Perhaps those alternatives are too extreme, but the loss seems to me of that magnitude.

Some readers are put off because the poem's beliefs – about religion, about relations between the sexes – are not ours. But that is true of most literature from the past. Literature educates because it requires us to inhabit a mind-set different from our own.

A likelier reason for the poem's neglect, I believe, is its length. Its twelve books total over 11,500 lines. Embarking on that seems a formidable undertaking, particularly at a time when narrative poems are not part of our habitual reading. My aim in this shortened version has been to preserve those passages that seem to me pre-eminent, not only for their poetic power, but also for their contribution to the poem's intellectual structure – what Milton called its 'great argument'. It will be objected that my decisions about what to select and what to omit are subjective, and that is true. But they also reflect my observation of what does, and what does not, arouse the eager interest of students during several decades of teaching and lecturing about the poem at Oxford.

Another objection is that any selection destroys the architecture of the poem and obscures the relations of its parts to the whole. That is true too. But it would be a more relevant objection if my purpose were to displace *Paradise Lost* and offer a substitute. That is far from my aim. My hope, rather, is that the obvious greatness of what I have selected will lure readers back to encounter the poem in its full epic stature. It is also worth pointing out that, although *The Essential Paradise Lost* reduces the poem to one third of its original length (on word-count it is now slightly shorter than George Orwell's novella *Animal Farm*), it is not just an anthology of favourite excerpts. It preserves the structure of the original, summarising the content of omitted passages as they occur, explaining Milton's ideas and innovations, and drawing attention to the critical disputes they have ignited.

I have modernised Milton's spelling, but mostly retained the light punctuation of the first edition, which encourages the voice to flow on from line to line. For Milton *Paradise Lost* was a voiced thing – he never saw it written down or printed – and it is still best read aloud.

How Was *Paradise Lost* Written?

Paradise Lost is singular in that unlike any other poem of comparable length it was composed while the poet was asleep. Milton tells us that it was dictated to him, at night or in the early morning, by his 'celestial patroness', the heavenly muse whom he calls Urania (Book 7:1–39; 9:20–4). Those close to Milton, including his widow, confirmed that this was how the poem came to be written. When he woke in the morning he would dictate sections of about forty lines to anyone available to write them down, and would then 'reduce them to half the number'. When he tried to write while awake he could not produce a single line.

Whether or not we believe in Urania, the fact that the poem was initially composed during sleep suggests that it came from Milton's unconscious, though when he woke it was revised by his conscious mind. In this respect it could be seen almost as two poems in one. There is an official poem, articulating ideas that are endorsed by Milton's conscious intention. Intersecting with it there is an unofficial poem, releasing disruptive meanings that Milton would not have consciously endorsed.

This divided authorship has, in turn, divided the poem's readers. Almost from the first there have been those who regard Satan, the official poem's villain, as the true hero, and recoil from Milton's God, who is officially the source of all goodness in the poem.

Like Satan, Milton was a rebel in a civil war, and a bitter foe of absolute monarchy. The idea that the epic expresses his unconscious hostility towards God was formulated, many years before

Freud developed his theory of the unconscious, by William Blake, who declared: 'The reason Milton wrote in fetters when he wrote of Angels & God, and at liberty when of Devils & Hell, is because he was a true Poet & of the Devil's party without knowing it.'

What Is *Paradise Lost* About?

The question *Paradise Lost* sets out to answer is, why is the world full of suffering? Modern readers might answer that question with reference to human nature – particularly its basic instincts, sex and aggression, which in the past served to ensure humanity's evolutionary survival, but now produce overpopulation and constant war.

Milton, too, blamed human nature. But as he was a seventeenth-century Christian his investigation into how human nature has evolved took him back to the beginning of time, as recorded in the Bible. The events of *Paradise Lost* are, in chronological order, God's creation of the universe, his creation of heaven and the angels who inhabit it, the rebellion of Satan and the wicked angels whom God throws into hell, and the creation of Adam and Eve, the first humans, who are tempted by Satan and fall and are turned out of Paradise.

However, Milton does not narrate these events in the order in which they supposedly happened. *Paradise Lost* starts in the middle, after Satan has been thrown into hell, and fills in the rest in flashbacks. In the last two books of the poem an angel gives Adam a summary of the future of the human race, just before turning him and Eve out of Paradise.

Milton's poem supplements the biblical account of man's fall and the events leading up to it by adding whole episodes which the Bible scarcely mentions, such as the war in heaven, or does not mention at all, such as Satan's character and speeches, the conversations between God and his Son, and the circumstances of Eve's and Adam's life together and of their temptations.

Why Was Milton Concerned about Human Suffering When Writing *Paradise Lost*?

Paradise Lost was written in the 1650s and early 1660s. These were disastrous years for Milton. His sight had begun to fail in the 1640s, and in 1652 he became totally blind. It seemed to him a wholly undeserved affliction and he cried out against divine injustice.

> *I call upon thee, my God, who knowest my inmost mind and all my thoughts, to witness that (although I have repeatedly examined myself on this point as earnestly as I could, and have searched all the corners of my life) I am conscious of nothing, or of no deed, either recent or remote, whose wickedness could justly occasion or invite upon me this supreme misfortune.*

This protest, written in 1653, helps us to see the Satan of *Paradise Lost*, with his resentment and his sense of 'injured merit'

THE ESSENTIAL PARADISE LOST

(1:98), as an outgrowth of Milton's own anguish. Another link with Satan relates specifically to blindness. The description of the hell into which Satan is cast, with its flashes of light and 'darkness visible', resembles Milton's description, in a letter written for a medical specialist, of the symptoms of his approaching blindness.

This is not to claim that Satan 'is' Milton. Milton rejected resentment and self-pity. Blindness made it improbable he would ever write the great epic poem that had been his ambition since youth, and in the sonnet on his blindness ('When I consider how my light is spent'), he records that his first impulse was to protest against God's unreasonableness in expecting him to go on writing, though blind:

> Doth God exact day-labour, light denied,
> I fondly ask?

But then he reminds himself that he and his ambitions are unnecessary to God.

> God doth not need
> Either man's works or his own gifts; who best
> Bear his mild yoke, they serve him best; his state
> Is kingly. Thousands at his bidding speed
> And post o'er land and ocean without rest:
> They also serve who only stand and wait.

So he did wait, and the great epic poem came to him 'unpremed-itated', as he relates (9:24), dictated each night by a divine female visitor.

The 1650s were grief-laden for Milton in other respects. Shortly after he went blind his wife died, and she was quickly followed to the grave by his son John, aged fifteen months. He married again, and his second wife, Katherine, bore him a daugh-ter. But both she and the child died within weeks of each other early in 1658. Katherine visited him at night too, in a dream, and he wrote a sonnet about it, 'Methought I saw my late-espoused saint.' Blind when they married, he had never seen her face, so in the dream it is hidden.

> *Her face was veiled, yet to my fancied sight*
> *Love, sweetness, goodness in her person shined*
> *So clear, as in no face with more delight.*
> *But O as to embrace me she inclined*
> *I waked, she fled, and day brought back my night.*

Added to these personal losses were national and political catastrophes. Despite his blindness, Milton had continued to work as Secretary for the Foreign Tongues for Cromwell's Council of State. At the Council's command he had written two Latin works for a European readership justifying the execution of Charles I. This put him in grave danger at the Restoration in 1660. Those who had signed Charles I's death warrant were rounded up and executed. Milton went into hiding, but was discovered, arrested and imprisoned. Though friends secured his release, his books were burned by the common hangman and he was subjected to threats and public ridicule. In the introduction to Book 7 of *Paradise Lost* he describes himself as 'fallen on evil days' and 'evil tongues'. The republican cause he had devoted himself to lay in ruins. As he saw it, the British people had turned their backs on freedom and chosen tyranny. *Paradise Lost* is written to show that their perversity, like all human ills, is traceable to the fall of man.

Is Satan the Hero?

Very few writers have attempted to depict absolute evil, and the character of Satan is often identified as the poem's great success. It seems that Satan was central to *Paradise Lost* from the start. According to Milton's nephew, the opening lines of Satan's soliloquy when he first alights on the earth (4:32–41) were written some years before the rest of the poem, when Milton was planning *Paradise Lost* as a drama, not an epic, and they were to be the opening lines of the drama.

However, it is easy to misread Satan. Shelley wrote:

Milton's Devil as a moral being is as far superior to his God, as one who perseveres in some purpose which he has conceived to be excellent, in spite of adversity and torture, is to one who in the cold security of undoubted triumph inflicts the most horrible revenge upon his enemy.

That is finely said, but it will not do. Satan does not conceive his purpose to be excellent. He knows that it is evil. His purpose is to destroy the innocent in order to spite God. He excuses himself for this as he watches Adam and Eve.

> *And should I at your harmless innocence*
> *Melt, as I do, yet public reason just,*
> *Honour and empire, with revenge enlarged,*
> *By conquering this new world, compels me now*
> *To do what else though damned I should abhor.*
> (4:388–92)

This is a terrorist's logic, and the Satan of *Paradise Lost* is English literature's first terrorist. Terrorism – the destruction of the innocent for political ends – was of interest to Milton. Two years before his birth the greatest terrorist atrocity ever planned in Britain, the Gunpowder Plot, was foiled. The plotters' intention had been to destroy the royal family and the entire British ruling class, gathered for the state opening of parliament. When he was in his teens Milton wrote six poems about it, all of them in Latin. In the longest he depicts Satan obtaining entry to the bedchamber of Pope Paul V and, whispering in his ear, suggesting the Gunpowder Plot to him while he sleeps. There are clear links between this poem and *Paradise Lost*, not least that, in the epic, Satan invents gunpowder.

Satan is not only a terrorist. Like many terrorists he is also a political leader. Milton was closer to the centre of British political life than any other poet has ever been. He saw how politicians behaved at times of national crisis, and the character of Satan grows from that observation. He shows that Satan's public and private selves are different. In public, before the mighty throng of his followers, Satan manipulates the levers of power with confidence, banishing self-doubt. He seems genuinely ignorant of facts – that God is invincible, that God created him – that when he is alone he acknowledges as unquestionably true. Milton's Satan is a study in the intoxication of leadership, and its capacity to numb parts of the brain that operate as a restraint in normal people.

When alone Satan is capable of pity – capable, at least momentarily, of becoming a quite different creature. This happens when he watches Eve in the garden.

> *That space the evil one abstracted stood*
> *From his own evil, and for the time remained*
> *Stupidly good; of enmity disarmed,*
> *Of guile, of hate, of envy, of revenge.*
>   (9:463–6)

It is an extraordinary moment – the most evil thing in creation ceases to be evil – and it shows that Satan could still relent. The tragedy need not happen. The mere sight of innocence disarms him and frees him from hatred.

Also extraordinary is Satan's earlier reaction when he first sees Adam and Eve and tries to work out what kind of beings they are:

Not spirits, yet to heavenly spirits bright
Little inferior; whom my thoughts pursue
With wonder, and could love, so lively shines
In them divine resemblance . . .
(4:361–4).

Satan says he could love the human pair *because they look like God*. But doesn't he hate God? Isn't God his enemy? Does Satan suddenly realise he loves God when he sees the human pair? Or have love and hatred of God furiously contested in him all along? We can't know. Satan is unfathomable, whereas *Paradise Lost's* God, being all-knowing, is as single-minded as a timetable, and cannot experience remorse and self-doubt as Satan does.

Milton's Muse

Milton's belief that *Paradise Lost* was divinely inspired has embarrassed some critics. But it is a claim unequivocally made in the poem itself. It is hard to say exactly how he imagined his Muse, whom he calls, provisionally, Urania (7:1–2). But it is clear that he thought she was female and very close to God. *Paradise Lost* claims that it was she who inspired Moses to write Genesis and the other Mosaic books of the Old Testament (1:6–10). That is to say, she is capable of dictating material that has biblical authority.

It is possible he thought *Paradise Lost* had biblical authority too. In his later poem, *Paradise Regained*, which he asks the same spirit to dictate, he claims that the events, though not recorded in the Bible, did really happen. They were:

> . . . *in secret done,*
> *And unrecorded left through many an age,*
> *Worthy t' have not remained so long unsung.*
> (*Paradise Regained*, Book 1:15–17)

That may be how he regarded the additions to scripture in *Paradise Lost*.

The closest Milton comes to identifying his Muse is at the start of Book 7 of *Paradise Lost*.

> *Before the hills appeared, or fountain flowed,*
> *Thou with eternal Wisdom didst converse,*
> *Wisdom thy sister, and with her didst play*
> *In presence of the almighty Father, pleased*
> *With thy celestial song.*
> (7: 8–12)

This draws on the biblical book of Proverbs, 8:25–7, 30, where Wisdom says that she existed with God before the creation of the world, and was 'daily his delight, rejoicing [Vulgate: *ludens*, playing] always before him'. The biblical Wisdom does not mention a sister, and how Milton knew his Muse was Wisdom's sister remains mysterious. The likeliest explanation seems to be that she told him herself.

Of course, many modern readers will dismiss Milton's belief in inspiration as an illusion. But whether we believe his poem was dictated to him by a supernatural female is less important than that he believed it himself. And since he did believe that, it seems reasonable to ask whether his listening, night after night, to a female voice dictating his poem to him may have influenced how femaleness is treated in the poem. Given that it was written by a female – or so he believed – is it in any sense a feminist poem?

That might seem unlikely, because the poem's subjection of Eve to Adam is officially endorsed as part of the divine plan. But *Paradise Lost* is a poem of more than one voice, and among the incidents that Milton's Muse adds to the scriptural account several lend themselves to feminist interpretation.

The most prominent is Eve's account of how, when she was first created, she was mistakenly attracted to her reflection in a pool, thinking it another being (Book 4:449–91). At the poem's official level this can easily be dismissed as a sign of Eve's female vanity, modelled on the Narcissus episode in Ovid. But there is another way of reading it. Eve is drawn to 'answering looks/Of sympathy and love' in the female face she sees. Then she hears God's voice telling her it is just a reflection, and ordering her to follow. Her function and destiny, God tells her, is to bear Adam's children:

> *. . . to him shalt bear*
> *Multitudes like thyself, and thence be called*
> *Mother of human race.*

But when she comes in sight of Adam her immediate reaction is revulsion. He looks 'Less winning soft, less amiably mild' than the reflection in the pool. So she turns round and heads back to the pool with Adam chasing after her and comically shouting in protest.

This is a completely new episode, inserted into the Bible story, and it makes it clear that Eve is not attracted by maleness (nor, perhaps, by God's hectoring instruction about the 'multitudes' she must give birth to). This may explain why, later, she wants to go gardening alone (9:205–389). She says it is because they will garden more efficiently that way, whereas when they are together they waste time on 'looks' and 'smiles' and 'casual discourse'. Adam is unwilling to let her go, and clearly enjoys the looks and smiles and casual discourse more than she does. Interestingly, Eve gets the better of the argument, although the poem's official line is that Adam is the more intelligent. He is afraid of offending her by telling her that he does not trust her to resist temptation by herself, so he pretends he thinks that for her to be tempted, even if she does not fall, will be a dishonour. Eve remains rational, quickly disposes of this silly idea and wins the argument.

Taken together, the pool episode and the argument in the garden bring a new female viewpoint to bear on the poem's events, and Eve also shows herself Adam's superior after the fall. When the human pair face their judge, Adam blusters, trying to shift the blame to Eve, and protesting that 'from her hand I could suspect no ill' (10:140), which is not true. Eve, by contrast, tells the truth without excuse: 'The serpent me beguiled and I did eat' (10:162).

When the pair are left alone together, Adam heaps blame and vilification on Eve, but it is Eve who sees what must be done. She says that she will return to the place of judgement and ask God to transfer all the punishment to her (10:933–5). Adam contemptuously dismisses this suggestion. 'If prayers/Could alter high decrees', he declares, he would get there before her and offer to take all the blame himself. In fact he had a chance to do this when confronting the judge, but was too terrified (10:133). But Eve's suggestion sets him thinking, and he comes to see that the right course is to return to the place of judgement and beg forgiveness. He no longer believes that prayers cannot alter high decrees. He now trusts God's mercy: 'Undoubtedly he will relent, and turn/ From his displeasure' (10:1093–4). It is, it turns out, a crucial decision. But it was Eve's better, female understanding of contrition and mercy that brought about the change.

Opinions will differ about whether Milton's female Muse was responsible for these proto-feminist changes to the Bible account. What is clear is that Milton thought she was.

The Style of *Paradise Lost*

To first-time readers the style of *Paradise Lost* is likely to come as a shock. That is the right reaction. Stylistically the poem is completely new. No previous writer had used English in such a way. The style was created in response to the demands of the subject.

Milton saw himself as the first to break silence about world-shaking events – 'Things unattempted yet in prose or rhyme' (1:16). To support his momentous revelations he fashioned what has come to be known as the Miltonic 'grand style'.

He explains (in a note prefaced to the poem) that he has chosen to write his epic in blank verse, rejecting rhyme, because 'the jingling sound of like endings' is 'trivial', and there is no place for triviality in his new style. To avoid triviality in vocabulary, he uses a high proportion of words of Latin derivation. This does not mean that he 'really' wrote Latin not English, nor need it make for obscurity. Many common English words derive from Latin, and some of the Latin-derived words that Milton coined in *Paradise Lost* have passed into common English usage ('terrific' and 'jubilant' are examples). But the echoes of Latin impart a classical gravity and authority, shifting the style away from the commonplace.

To add grandeur to the style Milton also introduces exotic proper names. They are often embedded in long similes, imitating Homer's use of similes in the *Iliad* and the *Odyssey*. The similes are not decorative. They reflect meanings into the narrative. But they also allow Milton to create magnificent sound effects that exist just as sound effects. He writes, for example, that Charlemagne's knights

> *Jousted in Aspramont or Montalban,*
> *Damasco, or Marocco, or Trebisond.*
> (1:583–4)

[16]

It would be hard to argue here that the place names are chosen for their precise geographical significance rather than for their sonorous splendour.

Paradise Lost's long sentences, with their many dependent clauses and side-turnings, were another stylistic innovation, and it, too, has been criticised as too much like Latin. But in fact their loose digressive shifts would be impossible in the tight grammatical structures of Latin. They are thoroughly English, and they enliven the poem with subtleties that traditional accounts of the grand style miss.

One of these subtleties is the run-over of meaning from phrase to phrase and line to line. It is what Milton described, in the note prefaced to the poem, as 'the sense variously drawn out from one verse into another'. At the end of one phrase or line the sense seems complete, only for the next to supplement or modify it. An example noticed by one of the earliest commentators on *Paradise Lost* comes in Adam's description of his first moments of consciousness after his creation:

> . . . *about me round I saw*
> *Hill, dale, and shady woods, and sunny plains,*
> *And liquid lapse of murmuring streams, by these*
> *Creatures that lived, and moved, and walked, or flew,*
> *Birds on the branches warbling; all things smiled*
> *With fragrance and with joy my heart o'erflowed.*
> (8:261–6)

It is impossible to say whether all things smiled with fragrance and joy, or whether Adam's heart overflowed with fragrance and joy, or whether some other permutation applies (nature smiling with fragrance, Adam's heart overflowing with joy, for example).

You may say it does not matter much. But think again. What the subtle merging of meanings shows is that Adam is at one with nature. He does not, or cannot, or does not care to distinguish between what is happening in nature and what is happening in his own heart. The same phrase does for both. The meanings slide into each other, and it is a mark of Adam's unfallen state that nature and his heart are one.

These lines also illustrate how the effect of the fall twists and alters words across wide stretches of the poem. The next time the word 'smiled' occurs in *Paradise Lost* is some 1200 lines later, when Adam, aghast, sees fallen Eve coming towards him through the trees: 'in her hand/A bough of fairest fruit, that downy smiled' (9:850–1). The world has fallen, and a word that signified nature's innocence has fallen too, becoming sinister and mocking.

A number of key words in the poem change in this way. Carrying no threat before the fall, they come to signify evil after it. 'Lapse' is one such word, occurring only twice in the poem. In Adam's joyful speech the 'liquid lapse' of the streams is as innocent as birdsong. After the fall, 'lapse' can no longer be used innocently. It comes to signify original sin, and the loss of man's freedom that goes with it, as the archangel Michael explains to

Adam: 'Since thy original lapse, true liberty/Is lost . . .' (12:83–4).

'Maze', 'error', 'serpent' and 'wandering' are other words that fall. When, at the creation, God separates land and water, the rivers, 'with serpent error wandering' (7:302) are innocent, so are the brooks in Paradise that run 'With mazy error under pendant shades' (4:239). But once sin has entered the world these words are overtaken by evil. The devils in hell debate philosophy, 'in wandering mazes lost' (2:361), and the pathos of the poem's ending is shadowed by the devilish associations of 'wandering':

> *They hand in hand with wandering steps and slow,*
> *Through Eden took their solitary way.*
>   (12:648–9)

Apart from the two humans, the poem's characters are not just colossal but unimaginable, and Milton incorporates this indistinctness into his descriptions. Here, for example, is Satan, at the start of the poem, heaving himself up from the burning lake in hell and making for the shore.

> *. . . his ponderous shield*
> *Ethereal temper, massy, large and round,*
> *Behind him cast; the broad circumference*
> *Hung on his shoulders like the moon, whose orb*
> *Through optic glass the Tuscan artist views*
> *At evening from the top of Fesole,*
> *Or in Valdarno, to descry new lands,*

Rivers or mountains in her spotty globe.
His spear, to equal which the tallest pine
Hewn on Norwegian hills, to be the mast
Of some great admiral, were but a wand,
He walked with to support uneasy steps
Over the burning marl . . .

(1:284–96)

Satan's shield starts by seeming quite real and solid ('massy, large and round'). But in the next line what hangs on his shoulders is not a shield but a 'circumference'. The shield has begun to fade. In the next line it is like the moon – and we think we know what that looks like. But this is the moon as seen by Galileo ('the Tuscan artist') through his telescope. So it is an enlarged moon. But enlarged how much? We can't tell precisely, not knowing how Galileo has fixed his focus. But within a couple of lines this is a shield with lands, rivers and mountains on it – way beyond imagining.

So too with Satan's spear. At first Milton seems to be saying that it is like the mast of a great flagship (a seventeenth-century meaning of 'admiral'). But then the last four words of the description – 'were but a wand' – fling that comparison away as totally inadequate, and we are left with no notion of the spear's vastness.

The lines about the spear are typical, in that the order in which Milton releases his words at us matters greatly – as much, say, as the order of visual images in a film. His is not a static art, but mobile, and constantly readjusting.

The comparison with film is too restrictive for Milton's art, though. He works on our visual sense, but just as often on other senses. Here is Raphael describing to Adam how a plant grows.

> *So from the root*
> *Springs lighter the green stalk, from thence the leaves*
> *More airy, last the bright consummate flower*
> *Spirits odorous breathes.*
> (5:479–82)

The plant is only vaguely seen. We can't even tell what colour it is. What is registered, rather, is the plant's mass. It is a kind of weight-picture, engaging our sense of tactile density and lightness. The bulky word 'consummate', balanced on the light stalk, seems too heavy, but 'spirits' and 'breathes' keep it fuming away into the air. We realise that Milton is getting across the contrast between the precarious size of the flower, relative to the stalk, and its filmy lightness, almost as insubstantial as a scent.

The substitution of hearing for sight is common, and reminds us that this is the work of a blind poet. When Eve asks Adam why the stars go on shining even when she and Adam are asleep, he tells her that they are not the world's only inhabitants: 'Millions of spiritual creatures walk the earth . . .' The line suggests shimmering angel-shapes, coming and going. But the start of the next line snatches that visual glimpse away. The spiritual creatures have never been seen. They are known only by sound:

Millions of spiritual creatures walk the earth
Unseen, both when we wake, and when we sleep:
All these with ceaseless praise his works behold
Both day and night: how often from the steep
Of echoing hill or thicket have we heard
Celestial voices to the midnight air,
Sole, or responsive to each other's note
Singing their great creator . . .
(4:677–84)

Milton's sensitivity to sound is so acute that he can use sound to change the way things look. An example is the description of the fig-tree in Eden. It has long, spreading branches that bend to the earth and take root, so that:

. . . daughters grow
About the mother tree, a pillared shade
High overarched, and echoing walks between . . .
(9:1105–7)

The last three words widen the vista. Suddenly it sounds more like a cathedral than a tree. But we hear the spaciousness, rather than seeing it. We are reminded of how the blind can use echo-location to orient themselves.

Satan's palace, Pandemonium, seems to be built by sound. We are told of the molten metals that go into its construction and the 'golden architrave' and other architectural marvels that it incorporates. Yet the actual building arises as if by magic.

> *Anon out of the earth a fabric huge*
> *Rose like an exhalation, with the sound*
> *Of dulcet symphonies and voices sweet.*
> (1:710–12)

Are we meant to realise that its seeming magnificence is as insubstantial as a breath? Or is it meant to remind us how much power and beauty the fallen angels still command? Or both?

As you would expect in a poem that hinges on eating an apple, taste and smell are alerted along with the other senses. When Satan first lands on earth the fragrance of Eden reaches him on the wind;

> *As when to them who sail*
> *Beyond the Cape of Hope, and now are past*
> *Mozambic, off at sea north-east winds blow*
> *Sabean odours from the spicy shore*
> *Of Araby the blest.*
> (4:159–63)

'Beyond the Cape of Hope' is double: a geographical location, but also a reminder that, despite Eden's fragrances, Satan is always in hell, where 'hope never comes' (1:66).

Satan arouses taste and smell when he tempts Eve. Disguised

as a snake, he finds her alone in the garden, and tells her how he
came upon the tree, laden with fruit:

> *I nearer drew to gaze;*
> *When from the boughs a savoury odour blown,*
> *Grateful to appetite, more pleased my sense*
> *Than smell of sweetest fennel, or the teats*
> *Of ewe or goat dropping with milk at even,*
> *Unsucked of lamb or kid, that tend their play.*
> *To satisfy the sharp desire I had*
> *Of tasting those fair apples, I resolved*
> *Not to defer.*
>   (9:578–87)

Does Satan imagine that the milk and teats are fragrant as well as
the fennel? We can't be sure. Taste and smell mingle and collude
in his imaginings.

Of course, he has made the whole thing up. Acting the part of a
snake, he remembers that snakes were supposed to like fennel and
to suck milk from sheep and goats. So he pretends that he does
as well. Really he has no interest in fennel, milk or apples. What
he is actually thinking about, we deduce, and what led him to
think about teats and milk in the first place, is the naked woman
standing before him. His eyes rove over her breasts, shamelessly
displayed, and they evoke desire. The normal word order would
be, 'I resolved not to defer to satisfy the sharp desire . . .' But he is
tormented by unsatisfied lust, so 'To satisfy the sharp desire' can't

wait, and thrusts itself to the start of the sentence in unguarded fierceness.

Satan's sensuous imaginings might surprise those who think of Milton as a puritan. But he is credited with coining the word 'sensuous', and he described poetry as 'simple, sensuous and passionate'. It is enriching, in reading *Paradise Lost*, to notice how the subtleties of its style continually enliven the senses.

PARADISE LOST

BOOK 1

Milton does not present Paradise Lost *as his own work. He begins his epic by asking the heavenly Muse to 'sing' his poem for him, and briefly sketches what its main events will be. Then (at line 54) the poem's narrative starts, with Satan, the leader of the angels who have rebelled against God, chained on a burning lake in hell and becoming aware of his new surroundings.*

Of man's first disobedience, and the fruit
Of that forbidden tree, whose mortal taste
Brought death into the world, and all our woe,
With loss of Eden, till one greater man
Restore us, and regain the blissful seat,   5
Sing heavenly Muse, that on the secret top
Of Oreb, or of Sinai, didst inspire
That shepherd, who first taught the chosen seed,
In the beginning how the heavens and earth
Rose out of chaos: or, if Sion hill   10
Delight thee more, and Siloa's brook that flowed
Fast by the oracle of God, I thence

4. *greater man.* Christ. 6. *Muse.* See 'Milton's Muse', p. 11–15. 8. *shepherd.* Moses, whom God spoke to on Mounts *Sinai* and *Oreb* (Horeb). 10. *Sion hill . . . Siloa's brook.* Sites in Jerusalem associated with divine inspiration. 12. *thence.* From there.

Invoke thy aid to my adventurous song,
That with no middle flight intends to soar
Above th' Aonian mount, while it pursues   15
Things unattempted yet in prose or rhyme.
And chiefly thou, O Spirit, that dost prefer
Before all temples the upright heart and pure,
Instruct me, for thou knowst; thou from the first
Wast present, and with mighty wings outspread,   20
Dovelike satst brooding on the vast abyss,
And mad'st it pregnant: what in me is dark
Illumine, what is low raise and support;
That to the height of this great argument
I may assert eternal providence,   25
And justify the ways of God to men.
Say first, for heaven hides nothing from thy view
Nor the deep tract of hell, say first what cause
Moved our grand parents in that happy state,
Favoured of heaven so highly, to fall off   30
From their creator, and transgress his will
For one restraint, lords of the world besides?
Who first seduced them to that foul revolt?
The infernal serpent; he it was whose guile,
Stirred up with envy and revenge, deceived   35

15. Aonian mount. Helicon, sacred to the pagan Muses. *17–22. Spirit . . . pregnant.*
The Holy Spirit appeared as a dove at Christ's baptism. But Milton's image of the
Spirit as a dove, hatching the universe, is not biblical.

The mother of mankind, what time his pride
Had cast him out from heaven, with all his host
Of rebel angels, by whose aid aspiring
To set himself in glory above his peers,
He trusted to have equalled the most high,   40
If he opposed; and with ambitious aim
Against the throne and monarchy of God
Raised impious war in heaven and battle proud,
With vain attempt. Him the almighty power
Hurled headlong flaming from the ethereal sky,   45
With hideous ruin and combustion down
To bottomless perdition, there to dwell
In adamantine chains and penal fire,
Who durst defy the omnipotent to arms.
Nine times the space that measures day and night   50
To mortal men, he with his horrid crew
Lay vanquished, rolling in the fiery gulf
Confounded though immortal: but his doom
Reserved him to more wrath; for now the thought
Both of lost happiness and lasting pain   55
Torments him: round he throws his baleful eyes
That witnessed huge affliction and dismay
Mixed with obdurate pride and steadfast hate;
At once, as far as angels' ken he views
The dismal situation waste and wild.   60
A dungeon horrible, on all sides round
As one great furnace flamed, yet from those flames

No light, but rather darkness visible
Served only to discover sights of woe,
Regions of sorrow, doleful shades, where peace 65
And rest can never dwell, hope never comes
That comes to all; but torture without end
Still urges, and a fiery deluge, fed
With ever-burning sulphur unconsumed;
Such place eternal justice had prepared 70
For those rebellious, here their prison ordained
In utter darkness, and their portion set,
As far removed from God and light of heaven
As from the centre thrice to the utmost pole.
Oh how unlike the place from whence they fell! 75
There the companions of his fall, o'erwhelmed
With floods and whirlwinds of tempestuous fire,
He soon discerns, and weltering by his side
One next himself in power, and next in crime,
Long after known in Palestine, and named 80
Beelzebub. To whom the arch-enemy,
And thence in heaven called Satan, with bold words
Breaking the horrid silence thus began.

If thou beest he; but oh how fallen! how changed
From him, who in the happy realms of light 85
Clothed with transcendent brightness didst outshine

74. *centre ... pole.* Three times the distance from the centre of the universe to its edge.
81. *Beelzebub.* A 'prince of the devils' in the Bible, and a Philistine god.

Myriads, though bright; if he whom mutual league,
United thoughts and counsels, equal hope
And hazard in the glorious enterprise,
Joined with me once, now misery hath joined   90
In equal ruin; into what pit thou seest
From what height fallen: so much the stronger proved
He with his thunder; and till then who knew
The force of those dire arms? Yet not for those
Nor what the potent victor in his rage   95
Can else inflict, do I repent or change,
Though changed in outward lustre, that fixed mind,
And high disdain, from sense of injured merit,
That with the mightiest raised me to contend,
And to the fierce contention brought along   100
Innumerable force of spirits armed
That durst dislike his reign, and me preferring,
His utmost power with adverse power opposed
In dubious battle on the plains of heaven,
And shook his throne. What though the field be lost? 105
All is not lost; the unconquerable will,
And study of revenge, immortal hate,
And courage never to submit or yield:
And what is else not to be overcome?
That glory never shall his wrath or might   110
Extort from me. To bow and sue for grace
With suppliant knee, and deify his power
Who from the terror of this arm so late

Doubted his empire, that were low indeed,
That were an ignominy and shame beneath   115
This downfall; since by fate the strength of gods
And this empyreal substance cannot fail,
Since through experience of this great event
In arms not worse, in foresight much advanced,
We may with more successful hope resolve   120
To wage by force or guile eternal war
Irreconcilable to our grand foe,
Who now triumphs, and in the excess of joy
Sole reigning holds the tyranny of heaven.

    So spake the apostate angel, though in pain,   125
Vaunting aloud, but racked with deep despair.

*Beelzebub's reply is defeatist. He now believes that God is invincible,
and fears the fallen angels may be kept in hell to work as God's slaves.
Satan responds defiantly:*

Fallen cherub, to be weak is miserable
Doing or suffering: but of this be sure,
To do aught good never will be our task,
But ever to do ill our sole delight,   160
As being the contrary to his high will
Whom we resist. If then his providence
Out of our evil seek to bring forth good,
Our labour must be to pervert that end,
And out of good still to find means of evil;   165

Which oft-times may succeed, so as perhaps
Shall grieve him, if I fail not, and disturb
His inmost counsels from their destined aim.
But see! the angry victor hath recalled
His ministers of vengeance and pursuit   170
Back to the gates of heaven: the sulphurous hail,
Shot after us in storm, o'erblown hath laid
The fiery surge, that from the precipice
Of heaven received us falling; and the thunder,
Winged with red lightning and impetuous rage,   175
Perhaps hath spent his shafts, and ceases now
To bellow through the vast and boundless deep.
Let us not slip the occasion, whether scorn,
Or satiate fury yield it from our foe.
Seest thou yon dreary plain, forlorn and wild,   180
The seat of desolation, void of light,
Save what the glimmering of these livid flames
Casts pale and dreadful? Thither let us tend
From off the tossing of these fiery waves,
There rest, if any rest can harbour there,   185
And reassembling our afflicted powers,
Consult how we may henceforth most offend
Our enemy, our own loss how repair,
How overcome this dire calamity,
What reinforcement we may gain from hope,   190
If not what resolution from despair.

Satan, Milton goes on to explain, would have stayed chained on the burning lake for ever if God had not intervened and allowed him to escape. The reader may feel this was remiss of God. But it is a salient feature of the God of Paradise Lost *that he allows his creatures free will. So Satan is permitted to carry out his evil intentions. Being all-knowing, God foresees that he will bring about the fall of Adam and Eve. However, as Milton points out, God also foresees that Satan, by escaping, will 'Heap on himself damnation', whereas man will be redeemed by God's 'Infinite goodness, grace and mercy'. So (at any rate from the point of view of the God of* Paradise Lost*), everything will be for the best.*

Rising from the burning lake, Satan and Beelzebub head for a region of hell that consists of solid rather than liquid fire. Both believe they have freed themselves through their own strength, not God's permission. Satan expresses his resentment and resolve.

Is this the region, this the soil, the clime,
Said then the lost archangel, this the seat
That we must change for heaven, this mournful gloom
For that celestial light? Be it so, since he   245
Who now is sovereign can dispose and bid
What shall be right: furthest from him is best
Whom reason hath equalled, force hath made supreme
Above his equals. Farewell happy fields
Where joy for ever dwells: hail horrors, hail   250
Infernal world, and thou profoundest hell,
Receive thy new possessor: one who brings

PARADISE LOST: BOOK 1

A mind not to be changed by place or time.
The mind is its own place, and in itself
Can make a heaven of hell, a hell of heaven.   255
What matter where, if I be still the same,
And what I should be, all but less than he
Whom thunder hath made greater? Here at least
We shall be free; the almighty hath not built
Here for his envy, will not drive us hence: 260
Here we may reign secure, and in my choice,
To reign is worth ambition, though in hell:
Better to reign in hell than serve in heaven.

Satan determines to arouse his army of fallen angels, who are still lying stunned on the lake of fire. Beelzebub, less defeatist now, says he is sure they will respond to Satan's call.

He scarce had ceased when the superior fiend
Was moving toward the shore; his ponderous shield
Ethereal temper, massy, large and round,   285
Behind him cast; the broad circumference
Hung on his shoulders like the moon, whose orb
Through optic glass the Tuscan artist views
At evening from the top of Fesole,
Or in Valdarno, to descry new lands,   290

288. *Tuscan artist.* Galileo, who, with his telescope, first observed mountains on the moon. Milton may have met him when in Italy. *289. Fesole.* Fiesole. *290. Valdarno.* The Arno valley.

Rivers or mountains in her spotty globe.
His spear, to equal which the tallest pine
Hewn on Norwegian hills, to be the mast
Of some great admiral, were but a wand,
He walked with to support uneasy steps   295
Over the burning marl, not like those steps
On heaven's azure, and the torrid clime
Smote on him sore besides, vaulted with fire;
Natheless he so endured, till on the beach
Of that inflamed sea he stood, and called   300
His legions, angel forms, who lay entranced
Thick as autumnal leaves that strew the brooks
In Vallombrosa, where the Etrurian shades
High overarched embower; or scattered sedge
Afloat, when the fierce winds Orion armed   305
Hath vexed the Red Sea coast, whose waves o'erthrew
Busiris and his Memphian chivalry,
While with perfidious hatred they pursued
The sojourners of Goshen, who beheld
From the safe shore their floating carcasses   310
And broken chariot wheels, so thick bestrewn,
Abject and lost lay these, covering the flood,
Under amazement of their hideous change.

294. *admiral.* Flagship. *303. Vallombrosa.* Valley near Florence. *Etrurian.* Italian.
305. Orion. Constellation associated with storms. *307–9. Busiris.* A pharoah. *Memphian.*
Egyptian. *sojourners of Goshen.* The Israelites, rescued by the parting of the Red Sea,
Exodus 14:21–9.

He called so loud, that all the hollow deep
Of hell resounded. Princes, potentates,   315
Warriors, the flower of heaven, once yours, now lost,
If such astonishment as this can seize
Eternal spirits: or have ye chosen this place
After the toil of battle to repose
Your wearied virtue, for the ease you find   320
To slumber here, as in the vales of heaven?
Or in this abject posture have ye sworn
To adore the conqueror, who now beholds
Cherub and seraph rolling in the flood
With scattered arms and ensigns, till anon   325
His swift pursuers from heaven gates discern
The advantage, and descending tread us down
Thus drooping, or with linked thunderbolts
Transfix us to the bottom of this gulf?
Awake, arise, or be for ever fallen.   330

The devils respond to Satan's call, and rally around his imperial ensign.

            . . . anon they move
In perfect phalanx to the Dorian mood   550
Of flutes and soft recorders, such as raised
To height of noblest temper heroes old
Arming to battle, and instead of rage

550. Dorian. One of the ancient musical modes.

[39]

Deliberate valour breathed, firm and unmoved
With dread of death to flight or foul retreat;   555
Nor wanting power to mitigate and swage
With solemn touches, troubled thoughts, and chase
Anguish and doubt and fear and sorrow and pain
From mortal or immortal minds. Thus they,
Breathing united force with fixed thought,   560
Moved on in silence to soft pipes that charmed
Their painful steps o'er the burnt soil, and now
Advanced in view they stand, a horrid front
Of dreadful length and dazzling arms, in guise
Of warriors old with ordered spear and shield,   565
Awaiting what command their mighty chief
Had to impose; he through the armed files
Darts his experienced eye, and soon traverse
The whole battalion views, their order due,
Their visages and stature as of gods,   570
Their number last he sums. And now his heart
Distends with pride, and hardening in his strength
Glories: for never since created man,
Met such embodied force, as named with these
Could merit more than that small infantry   575
Warred on by cranes: though all the giant brood
Of Phlegra with the heroic race were joined

556. *swage*. Assuage. 563. *horrid*. In its Latin sense, bristling (with weapons). 575.
infantry. Pygmies, warred on by cranes in Greek myth. 577. *Phlegra*. Where giants
warred with gods in classical myth.

That fought at Thebes and Ilium, on each side
Mixed with auxiliar gods; and what resounds
In fable or romance of Uther's son   580
Begirt with British and Armoric knights,
And all who since, baptised or infidel
Jousted in Aspramont or Montalban,
Damasco, or Marocco, or Trebisond,
Or whom Biserta sent from Afric shore   585
When Charlemain with all his peerage fell
By Fontarabbia. Thus far these beyond
Compare of mortal prowess, yet observed
Their dread commander: he above the rest
In shape and gesture proudly eminent   590
Stood like a tower; his form had yet not lost
All her original brightness, nor appeared
Less than archangel ruined, and the excess
Of glory obscured: as when the sun new ris'n
Looks through the horizontal misty air   595
Shorn of his beams, or from behind the moon
In dim eclipse disastrous twilight sheds
On half the nations, and with fear of change
Perplexes monarchs. Darkened so, yet shone

578. Thebes . . . Ilium. Sites of heroic struggle in classical epics. *580. Uther's son.* King
Arthur. *Armoric.* From Brittany. *583–5. Aspramont, Montalban, Damasco* (Damascus),
Marocco (Marrakech), *Trebisond* and *Bizerta* feature in epic accounts of Charlemagne's
battles against the Saracens. *586. Charlemain.* In fact not Charlemagne but Roland,
one of his 'peers', fell in battle at Roncevalles, near *Fontarabbia* (Fuentarrabia).

Above them all the archangel: but his face   600
Deep scars of thunder had intrenched, and care
Sat on his faded cheek, but under brows
Of dauntless courage, and considerate pride
Waiting revenge: cruel his eye, but cast
Signs of remorse and passion to behold   605
The fellows of his crime, the followers rather
(Far other once beheld in bliss) condemned
For ever now to have their lot in pain,
Millions of spirits for his fault amerced
Of heaven, and from eternal splendours flung   610
For his revolt, yet faithful how they stood,
Their glory withered. As, when heaven's fire
Hath scathed the forest oaks, or mountain pines,
With singed top their stately growth, though bare,
Stands on the blasted heath. He now prepared   615
To speak; whereat their doubled ranks they bend
From wing to wing, and half enclose him round
With all his peers: attention held them mute.
Thrice he assayed, and thrice in spite of scorn,
Tears such as angels weep, burst forth: at last   620
Words interwove with sighs found out their way.
    O myriads of immortal spirits, O powers
Matchless, but with the almighty, and that strife
Was not inglorious, though the event was dire,

609. *amerced.* Deprived.

As this place testifies, and this dire change,   625
Hateful to utter: but what power of mind,
Foreseeing or presaging, from the depth
Of knowledge past or present, could have feared
How such united force of gods, how such
As stood like these, could ever know repulse?   630
For who can yet believe, though after loss,
That all these puissant legions, whose exile
Hath emptied heaven, shall fail to re-ascend,
Self-raised, and repossess their native seat?
For me be witness all the host of heaven,   635
If counsels different, or danger shunned
By me, have lost our hopes. But he who reigns
Monarch in heaven, till then as one secure
Sat on his throne, upheld by old repute,
Consent or custom, and his regal state   640
Put forth at full, but still his strength concealed,
Which tempted our attempt, and wrought our fall.
Henceforth his might we know, and know our own
So as not either to provoke, or dread
New war provoked; our better part remains   645
To work in close design, by fraud or guile,
What force effected not: that he no less
At length from us may find, who overcomes

629. *gods*. Referring to angels as 'gods' is biblical, as in Psalm 8:5. Satan never calls
God 'God'.

By force, hath overcome but half his foe.
Space may produce new worlds; whereof so rife   650
There went a fame in heaven that he ere long
Intended to create, and therein plant
A generation, whom his choice regard
Should favour equal to the sons of heaven:
Thither, if but to pry, shall be perhaps   655
Our first eruption, thither or elsewhere:
For this infernal pit shall never hold
Celestial spirits in bondage, nor the abyss
Long under darkness cover. But these thoughts
Full counsel must mature: peace is despaired;   670
For who can think submission? War then, war
Open or understood must be resolved.

*Inspired by Satan's rhetoric, his warriors hurl defiance at heaven. They
discover 'metallic ore' under hell's fiery surface and use it to build a
palace, called Pandemonium.*

Anon out of the earth a fabric huge   710
Rose like an exhalation, with the sound
Of dulcet symphonies and voices sweet,
Built like a temple, where pilasters round
Were set, and Doric pillars overlaid
With golden architrave; nor did there want   715
Cornice or frieze, with bossy sculptures graven,
The roof was fretted gold. Not Babylon

Nor great Alcairo such magnificence
Equalled in all their glories, to enshrine
Belus or Serapis their gods, or seat   720
Their kings, when Egypt with Assyria strove
In wealth and luxury. The ascending pile
Stood fixed her stately height, and straight the doors,
Opening their brazen folds discover wide
Within, her ample spaces o'er the smooth   725
And level pavement: from the arched roof,
Pendent by subtle magic many a row
Of starry lamps and blazing cressets fed
With naphtha and asphaltus yielded light
As from a sky. The hasty multitude   730
Admiring entered; and the work some praise
And some the architect: his hand was known
In heaven by many a towered structure high,
Where sceptred angels held their residence,
And sat as princes, whom the supreme king   735
Exalted to such power, and gave to rule,
Each in his hierarchy, the orders bright.
Nor was his name unheard or unadored
In ancient Greece; and in Ausonian land
Men called him Mulciber; and how he fell   740

718. *Alcairo.* Memphis (modern Cairo). *720. Belus.* The Babylonian god Baal.
Serapis. An Egyptian god. *739. Ausonian land.* Italy. *740. Mulciber.* The Greek god of
metal-work, Hephaistos.

From heaven, they fabled, thrown by angry Jove
Sheer o'er the crystal battlements: from morn
To noon he fell, from noon to dewy eve,
A summer's day; and with the setting sun
Dropped from the zenith, like a falling star,   745
On Lemnos th' Aegaean isle: thus they relate,
Erring; for he with this rebellious rout
Fell long before; nor aught availed him now
To have built in heaven high towers; nor did he scape
By all his engines, but was headlong sent   750
With his industrious crew to build in hell.

Satan's heralds announce a solemn council to be held in Pandemonium.
The fallen angels gather, and their leaders, the 'great seraphic lords and
cherubim', hold a debate, related in Book 2.

BOOK 2

High on a throne of royal state, which far
Outshone the wealth of Ormus and of Ind,
Or where the gorgeous East with richest hand
Showers on her kings barbaric pearl and gold,
Satan exalted sat, by merit raised   5
To that bad eminence; and from despair
Thus high uplifted beyond hope, aspires
Beyond thus high, insatiate to pursue
Vain war with heaven; and, by success untaught,
His proud imaginations thus displayed.   10
    Powers and dominions, deities of heaven,
For since no deep within her gulf can hold
Immortal vigour, though oppressed and fallen,
I give not heaven for lost. From this descent
Celestial virtues rising, will appear   15
More glorious and more dread than from no fall,
And trust themselves to fear no second fate:
Me though just right, and the fixed laws of heaven,
Did first create your leader, next, free choice,
With what besides, in council or in fight,   20

2. *Ormus.* Ormuz in the Persian Gulf, a centre for luxury trades. *Ind.* India. *9. success.*
In the Latin sense of 'outcome'.

[47]

Hath been achieved of merit, yet this loss,
Thus far at least recovered, hath much more
Established in a safe unenvied throne
Yielded with full consent. The happier state
In heaven, which follows dignity, might draw   25
Envy from each inferior; but who here
Will envy whom the highest place exposes
Foremost to stand against the thunderer's aim
Your bulwark, and condemns to greatest share
Of endless pain? Where there is then no good   30
For which to strive, no strife can grow up there
From faction: for none sure will claim in hell
Precedence; none, whose portion is so small
Of present pain, that with ambitious mind
Will covet more. With this advantage then   35
To union, and firm faith, and firm accord,
More than can be in heaven, we now return
To claim our just inheritance of old,
Surer to prosper than prosperity
Could have assured us; and by what best way,   40
Whether of open war or covert guile,
We now debate: who can advise, may speak.

The leading devils have their say. Moloch favours open war, arguing that, though they may lose, nothing could be worse than what they now suffer. Belial disagrees, pointing out that God may annihilate them if they are defeated.

And that must end us, that must be our cure, 145
To be no more; sad cure; for who would lose,
Though full of pain, this intellectual being,
Those thoughts that wander through eternity,
To perish rather, swallowed up and lost
In the wide womb of uncreated night, 150
Devoid of sense and motion?

Besides, Belial adds, God would be unlikely to grant them anything
as merciful as annihilation. He could devise punishments much worse
than what they now suffer.

War therefore, open or concealed, alike
My voice dissuades; for what can force or guile
With him, or who deceive his mind, whose eye
Views all things at one view? He from heaven's height 190
All these our motions vain sees and derides,
Not more almighty to resist our might
Than wise to frustrate all our plots and wiles.
Shall we then live thus vile, the race of heaven
Thus trampled, thus expelled, to suffer here 195
Chains and these torments? Better these than worse
By my advice; since fate inevitable
Subdues us, and omnipotent decree,
The victor's will. To suffer, as to do,
Our strength is equal; nor the law unjust 200
That so ordains.

Belial concludes that if they submit God may relent and, in time, lessen
their punishment.

Mammon speaks next. Like Belial he is against open war, because
they have no chance of defeating God. But he finds the idea that they
should accept God's mercy abhorrent.

   Suppose he should relent
And publish grace to all, on promise made
Of new subjection; with what eyes could we
Stand in his presence humble, and receive   240
Strict laws imposed, to celebrate his throne
With warbled hymns, and to his godhead sing
Forced alleluias, while he lordly sits
Our envied sovereign, and his altar breathes
Ambrosial odours and ambrosial flowers,   245
Our servile offerings? This must be our task
In heaven, this our delight; how wearisome
Eternity so spent in worship paid
To whom we hate.

Life in hell is not so bad, Mammon argues. They have discovered gold,
so can create 'magnificence' for themselves. True, it is dark in hell, but
when God was angry it was sometimes dark in heaven.

   This deep world
Of darkness do we dread? How oft amidst
Thick clouds and dark doth heaven's all-ruling sire

Choose to reside, his glory unobscured,   265
And with the majesty of darkness round
Covers his throne, from whence deep thunders roar
Mustering their rage, and heaven resembles hell?

*Mammon adds that they may in time get used to the pains of hell. So
he dismisses both Moloch's call to war and Belial's hope of reconciliation
with God. He advises that they remain true to themselves and make
the best of things where they are. This meets with general approval
among the devils.*

*However, Beelzebub, who speaks last in the debate, rejects both the
possibility of winning a war against God and the hope of remaining
peacefully in hell. They will always, he points out, be in God's power,
subject to what he chooses to inflict. He reminds them that it was well
known in heaven, before they were thrown out, that God intended
to create a new race called man. To revenge themselves on God they
should, he suggests, seek out this new race and either destroy them or
turn them against God. Milton explains that this idea, though voiced
by Beelzebub, originated with Satan. The devils receive the suggestion
with enthusiasm, and Beelzebub congratulates them on their wisdom.
However, he points out, they need a volunteer.*

But first, whom shall we send
In search of this new world, whom shall we find
Sufficient? Who shall tempt with wandering feet

---

265. unobscured. The darkness that does not obscure God's glory is from Psalm 18:11–13.

The dark unbottomed infinite abyss,   405
And through the palpable obscure find out
His uncouth way, or spread his airy flight,
Upborne with indefatigable wings
Over the vast abrupt, ere he arrive
The happy Isle; what strength, what art can then   410
Suffice, or what evasion bear him safe
Through the strict sentries and stations thick
Of angels watching round? Here he had need
All circumspection: and we now no less
Choice in our suffrage; for on whom we send   415
The weight of all and our last hope, relies.

The devils are all terrified. No one volunteers, until Satan rises and
offers to undertake the hazardous assignment himself. At this there is
general relief in hell, and the meeting breaks up.

The Stygian council thus dissolved, and forth
In order came the grand infernal peers,
Midst came their mighty paramount, and seemed
Alone the antagonist of heaven, nor less
Than hell's dread emperor, with pomp supreme,   510
And God-like imitated state; him round
A globe of fiery seraphim enclosed
With bright emblazonry, and horrent arms.

415. Choice . . . suffrage. Care in our election.

Then of their session ended they bid cry
With trumpets' regal sound the great result: 515
Toward the four winds four speedy cherubim
Put to their mouths the sounding alchemy,
By herald's voice explained; the hollow abyss
Heard far and wide, and all the host of hell
With deafening shout returned them loud acclaim.   520

While Satan is absent on his mission the remaining devils amuse them-
selves with various pastimes. Some engage in athletics, 'as at the
Olympian games':

  Others, more mild,
Retreated in a silent valley, sing
With notes angelical to many a harp
Their own heroic deeds, and hapless fall
By doom of battle; and complain that fate   550
Free virtue should enthral to force or chance.
Their song was partial, but the harmony
(What could it less when spirits immortal sing?)
Suspended hell, and took with ravishment
The thronging audience. In discourse more sweet   555
(For eloquence the soul, song charms the sense)

---

515. result. Of the debate. *517. alchemy.* Brass. *550–1. fate . . . enthral.* Inverted word
order. The normal order would be 'fate should enthral free virtue'. *552. partial.*
Prejudiced. *556. eloquence . . . sense.* Inversion. The normal word order would be
'eloquence charms the soul, song charms the sense'.

Others apart sat on a hill retired,
In thoughts more elevate, and reasoned high
Of providence, foreknowledge, will, and fate,
Fixed fate, free will, foreknowledge absolute,   560
And found no end, in wandering mazes lost.

*Whether God's foreknowledge can be reconciled with his creatures' free
will is a key question in the poem. So it is fitting that the devils should
discuss it and find it, as many of Milton's critics do, bewildering.*

*Other devils explore the terrain of hell and view with 'shuddering
horror' the torments that God has created for 'the damned' – that is, for
human beings in the future who, condemned by God, will spend eternity in hell. Meanwhile Satan starts his flight to the earth.*

Meanwhile the adversary of God and man,
Satan with thoughts inflamed of highest design,   630
Puts on swift wings, and toward the gates of hell
Explores his solitary flight: sometimes
He scours the right hand coast, sometimes the left,
Now shaves with level wing the deep, then soars
Up to the fiery concave towering high.   635
As when far off at sea a fleet descried
Hangs in the clouds, by equinoctial winds
Close sailing from Bengala, or the isles
Of Ternate and Tidore, whence merchants bring

637. Hangs in the clouds. Like a mirage.

Their spicy drugs; they on the trading flood   640
Through the wide Ethiopian to the Cape,
Ply stemming nightly toward the pole. So seemed
Far off the flying fiend.

At the gateway out of hell, Satan meets two allegorical beings, Sin and
Death. Sin has a woman's shape above the waist, but below she is a
serpent with a deadly sting. She is surrounded by a pack of hell-hounds
who, if disturbed, creep into her womb and hide there, barking and
howling.

Death is a spectral horror, indistinct except that 'what seems his
head' wears what looks like a 'kingly crown'. He and Satan are about
to fight, but Sin intervenes to stop them, crying out that Satan and
Death are father and son.

She proceeds to tell a strange story of events in heaven before the
evil angels fell, events of which Satan apparently has no recollection.
She says that when Satan first conspired against God, she sprang
fully armed out of his head. All the heavenly host recoiled in terror,
and named her Sin. However, the rebel angels were won over by her
beauty, especially her father, Satan, and she became pregnant by him.
Ejected from heaven with the rebel angels, she gave birth to Death.
His birth distorted her lower body into the serpent shape it now has.
Once born, Death pursued and raped her, begetting the hell-hounds

638–41. Spice ships from *Bengala* (Bengal) and the Moluccas or Indonesian spice
islands, *Ternate* and *Tidore*, would cross the *Ethiopian* Sea (Indian Ocean) before
rounding the *Cape* of Good Hope and heading north to Europe.

that now torment her by constantly entering and exiting her womb and gnawing her bowels.

There has been a lot of critical dispute about why Milton included this gruesome parody of motherhood and childbirth in his poem. None of the suggestions seems convincing. One effect of the episode is to associate Satan with sexual perversion as well as with pride and rebellion. That Satan's fall had a sexual component also relates it to Adam's fall.

Replying to Sin's revelations, Satan adopts a conciliatory tone, greeting her as his 'dear daughter' and Death as his 'fair son'. He explains that his mission, if successful, will benefit them because they will be able to leave hell and find prey in the new world God has created. They are both gleeful at the prospect, and Sin, who has been entrusted by God with the key to hell, unlocks the gate.

Beyond lies a vast emptiness called Chaos. This is what remains of the raw material that God used to create heaven, earth and hell. Satan pauses on the edge of this void before attempting to fly through it.

Into this wild abyss,   910
The womb of nature and perhaps her grave,
Of neither sea, nor shore, nor air, nor fire,
But all these in their pregnant causes mixed
Confusedly, and which thus must ever fight,
Unless the almighty maker them ordain   915
His dark materials to create more worlds,
Into this wild abyss the wary fiend
Stood on the brink of hell and looked a while,

Pondering his voyage; for no narrow frith
He had to cross.   920

Milton represents the rulers of this region as another pair of allegor-
ical beings, called Chaos and Night. They are suspicious of Satan, and
resent God's creation of heaven, earth and hell because it encroaches on
their kingdom of unformed matter. Satan assures them that he hopes
to reduce earth to its original darkness. Won over, Chaos gives Satan
directions for finding the earth, and he continues his perilous flight
through the dark.

But now at last the sacred influence
Of light appears, and from the walls of heaven   1035
Shoots far into the bosom of dim Night
A glimmering dawn; here nature first begins
Her farthest verge, and Chaos to retire,
As from her outmost works, a broken foe,
With tumult less, and with less hostile din;   1040
That Satan with less toil, and now with ease,
Wafts on the calmer wave by dubious light,
And like a weather-beaten vessel holds
Gladly the port, though shrouds and tackle torn;
Or in the emptier waste, resembling air,   1045
Weighs his spread wings, at leisure to behold
Far off the empyreal heaven, extended wide

919. frith. Firth. *1043. holds.* Reaches. *1046. Weighs.* Balances.

In circuit, undetermined square or round,
With opal towers and battlements adorned
Of living sapphire, once his native seat;   1050
And fast by hanging in a golden chain
This pendent world, in bigness as a star
Of smallest magnitude close by the moon.
Thither full fraught with mischievous revenge,
Accursed, and in a cursed hour he hies.   1055

1048. undetermined. Because heaven's vastness obscures its shape, or perhaps because earthly dimensions no longer apply. *1052. world.* The created universe. *1055. hies.* Hurries.

BOOK 3

As Satan arrives in sight of the earth the action of the poem moves into the light, leaving the darkness of hell and chaos behind. Milton starts Book 3 by addressing light and lamenting his blindness.

Hail, holy light, offspring of heaven first-born,
Or of the eternal co-eternal beam
May I express thee unblamed? since God is light,
And never but in unapproached light
Dwelt from eternity, dwelt then in thee,   5
Bright effluence of bright essence increate.
Or hearst thou rather pure ethereal stream,
Whose fountain who shall tell? Before the sun,
Before the heavens thou wert, and at the voice
Of God, as with a mantle didst invest   10
The rising world of waters dark and deep,
Won from the void and formless infinite.
Thee I revisit now with bolder wing,
Escaped the Stygian pool, though long detained

---

3. unblamed. Without incurring blame for suggesting that light may be eternal, whereas Christians believe only God is eternal.   *6. increate.* Uncreated (because eternal, like God, Milton suggests).   *7. hearst thou rather.* Would you rather be called?   *14. Stygian.* Relating to the Styx, a river in the classical underworld.

In that obscure sojourn, while in my flight   15
Through utter and through middle darkness borne
With other notes than to the Orphean lyre
I sung of Chaos and eternal Night;
Taught by the heavenly Muse to venture down
The dark descent, and up to re-ascend,   20
Though hard and rare: thee I revisit safe,
And feel thy sovereign vital lamp; but thou
Revisit'st not these eyes, that roll in vain
To find thy piercing ray, and find no dawn;
So thick a drop serene hath quenched their orbs,   25
Or dim suffusion veiled. Yet not the more
Cease I to wander where the Muses haunt
Clear spring, or shady grove, or sunny hill,
Smit with the love of sacred song; but chief
Thee Sion and the flowery brooks beneath,   30
That wash thy hallowed feet, and warbling flow,
Nightly I visit, nor sometimes forget
Those other two equalled with me in fate,
So were I equalled with them in renown,
Blind Thamyris and blind Maeonides,   35
And Tiresias and Phineus prophets old.

16. *utter*. Outer.   17. *Orphean*. The mythical lyre-player Orpheus entered the
underworld to rescue his wife Eurydice.   25. *drop serene*. Translating '*gutta serena*',
the seventeenth-century term for Milton's type of blindness.   30. *Sion*. See Book
1:10 note.   35–6. *Thamyris*, a legendary Thracian poet, *Maeonides* (Homer), *Tiresias*, a
prophet of Apollo, and *Phineus*, prophet and king of Thrace, were all blind.

Then feed on thoughts, that voluntary move
Harmonious numbers; as the wakeful bird
Sings darkling, and in shadiest covert hid
Tunes her nocturnal note. Thus with the year   40
Seasons return, but not to me returns
Day, or the sweet approach of even or morn,
Or sight of vernal bloom, or summer's rose,
Or flocks, or herds, or human face divine;
But cloud instead, and ever-during dark   45
Surrounds me, from the cheerful ways of men
Cut off, and for the book of knowledge fair
Presented with a universal blank
Of nature's works to me expunged and razed,
And wisdom at one entrance quite shut out.   50
So much the rather thou, celestial light,
Shine inward, and the mind through all her powers
Irradiate, there plant eyes, all mist from thence
Purge and disperse, that I may see and tell
Of things invisible to mortal sight.   55

The scene shifts to heaven, where the Son is seated next to God the Father. From this vantage point God can see Adam and Eve in the Garden of Eden, and Satan flying up towards the earth. He can also see the whole of time ('past, present, future he beholds'), and proceeds to tell the Son what the future holds.

38. bird. Nightingale.

Only begotten Son, seest thou what rage   80
Transports our adversary whom no bounds
Prescribed, no bars of hell, nor all the chains
Heaped on him there, nor yet the main abyss
Wide interrupt can hold; so bent he seems
On desperate revenge, that shall redound   85
Upon his own rebellious head. And now
Through all restraint broke loose he wings his way
Not far off heaven, in the precincts of light,
Directly towards the new created world,
And man there placed, with purpose to assay   90
If him by force he can destroy, or worse,
By some false guile pervert; and shall pervert;
For man will hearken to his glozing lies,
And easily transgress the sole command,
Sole pledge of his obedience: so will fall   95
He and his faithless progeny: whose fault?
Whose but his own? Ingrate, he had of me
All he could have; I made him just and right,
Sufficient to have stood, though free to fall.
Such I created all the ethereal powers   100
And spirits, both them who stood and them who failed;
Freely they stood who stood, and fell who fell.
Not free, what proof could they have given sincere
Of true allegiance, constant faith or love?
Where only what they needs must do appeared,   105
Not what they would, what praise could they receive?

What pleasure I from such obedience paid,
When will and reason (reason also is choice)
Useless and vain, of freedom both despoiled,
Made passive both, had served necessity,   110
Not me. They therefore, as to right belonged,
So were created, nor can justly accuse
Their maker, or their making, or their fate;
As if predestination overruled
Their will, disposed by absolute decree   115
Or high foreknowledge; they themselves decreed
Their own revolt, not I: if I foreknew,
Foreknowledge had no influence on their fault,
Which had no less proved certain unforeknown.
So without least impulse or shadow of fate,   120
Or aught by me immutably foreseen,
They trespass, authors to themselves in all
Both what they judge and what they choose; for so
I formed them free: and free they must remain,
Till they enthral themselves; I else must change   125
Their nature, and revoke the high decree
Unchangeable, eternal, which ordained
Their freedom; they themselves ordained their fall.
The first sort by their own suggestion fell,

106. would. Wished. *114. predestination.* The doctrine, adopted by Calvin but rejected
by Milton, that God destines some souls to damnation even before they are created.
129. first sort. Angels.

Self-tempted, self-depraved: man falls, deceived   130
By the other first: man therefore shall find grace,
The other none: in mercy and justice both,
Through heaven and earth, so shall my glory excel,
But mercy first and last shall brightest shine.

*The Son praises his Father for this promise of mercy, and – as if fearing
that the promise might be revoked – he urges that man should not be
utterly lost ('That be from thee far, / That far be from thee, Father').
He adds that if God were to 'abolish' the human race his goodness and
greatness would be questioned.*

    To whom the great creator thus replied.
O Son, in whom my soul hath chief delight,
Son of my bosom, Son who art alone
My word, my wisdom, and effectual might,   170
All hast thou spoken as my thoughts are, all
As my eternal purpose hath decreed;
Man shall not quite be lost, but saved who will,
Yet not of will in him, but grace in me
Freely vouchsafed; once more I will renew   175
His lapsed powers, though forfeit and enthralled
By sin to foul exorbitant desires;
Upheld by me, yet once more he shall stand

---

130. *self-tempted.* That is, tempted by one of their own kind. *174. grace.* In Christian
belief, fallen man is incapable of goodness, but God's *grace* makes him redeemable.

On even ground against his mortal foe,
By me upheld, that he may know how frail   180
His fallen condition is, and to me owe
All his deliverance, and to none but me.
Some I have chosen of peculiar grace
Elect above the rest; so is my will:
The rest shall hear me call, and oft be warned   185
Their sinful state, and to appease betimes
The incensed Deity, while offered grace
Invites; for I will clear their senses dark,
What may suffice, and soften stony hearts
To pray, repent, and bring obedience due.   190
To prayer, repentance, and obedience due,
Though but endeavoured with sincere intent,
Mine ear shall not be slow, mine eye not shut.
And I will place within them as a guide
My umpire conscience, whom if they will hear,   195
Light after light well used they shall attain,
And to the end persisting, safe arrive.
This my long sufferance and my day of grace,
They who neglect and scorn, shall never taste;
But hard be hardened, blind be blinded more,   200
That they may stumble on, and deeper fall;
And none but such from mercy I exclude.

183. *Some . . . peculiar grace.* In *Christian Doctrine* Milton wrote, 'God does not consider everyone worthy of equal grace and the cause of this is his supreme will.'

But yet all is not done; man disobeying,
Disloyal breaks his fealty, and sins
Against the high supremacy of heaven,   205
Affecting godhead, and so, losing all,
To expiate his treason hath nought left,
But to destruction sacred and devote,
He with his whole posterity must die,
Die he or justice must; unless for him   210
Some other able, and as willing, pay
The rigid satisfaction, death for death.
Say, heavenly powers, where shall we find such love,
Which of ye will be mortal to redeem
Man's mortal crime, and just the unjust to save,   215
Dwells in all heaven charity so dear?
He asked, but all the heavenly choir stood mute,
And silence was in heaven: on man's behalf
Patron or intercessor none appeared,
Much less that durst upon his own head draw   220
The deadly forfeiture, and ransom set.
And now without redemption all mankind
Must have been lost, adjudged to death and hell
By doom severe, had not the Son of God,
In whom the fullness dwells of love divine,   225
His dearest mediation thus renewed.
Father, thy word is past, man shall find grace;

204. *fealty.* Fidelity.   208. *sacred and devote.* Reserved for and assigned to.

And shall grace not find means, that finds her way,
The speediest of thy winged messengers
To visit all thy creatures, and to all   230
Comes unprevented, unimplored, unsought,
Happy for man, so coming; he her aid
Can never seek, once dead in sins and lost;
Atonement for himself or offering meet,
Indebted and undone, hath none to bring;   235
Behold me then: me for him, life for life
I offer: on me let thine anger fall;
Account me man; I for his sake will leave
Thy bosom, and this glory next to thee
Freely put off, and for him lastly die   240
Well pleased, on me let Death wreak all his rage;
Under his gloomy power I shall not long
Lie vanquished; thou hast given me to possess
Life in myself for ever, by thee I live,
Though now to Death I yield, and am his due,   245
All that of me can die, yet that debt paid,
Thou wilt not leave me in the loathsome grave
His prey, nor suffer my unspotted soul
For ever with corruption there to dwell;
But I shall rise victorious, and subdue   250
My vanquisher, spoiled of his vaunted spoil;
Death his death's wound shall then receive, and stoop

231. unprevented. Unasked beforehand.

[67]

Inglorious, of his mortal sting disarmed.
I through the ample air in triumph high
Shall lead hell captive maugre hell, and show   255
The powers of darkness bound. Thou at the sight
Pleased, out of heaven shalt look down and smile,
While by thee raised I ruin all my foes,
Death last, and with his carcass glut the grave:
Then with the multitude of my redeemed   260
Shall enter heaven, long absent, and return,
Father, to see thy face, wherein no cloud
Of anger shall remain, but peace assured
And reconcilement; wrath shall be no more
Thenceforth, but in thy presence joy entire.   265

*God the Father accepts the Son's offer of self-sacrifice, and says that
it shows he is 'By merit more than birth-right Son of God'. He tells
the Son, in the presence of the heavenly host, what the future holds.
The Son will die to save mankind, then re-ascend to heaven and
reign with God the Father. Then will come the Last Judgement,
when the Son will judge 'Bad men and angels'. Hell will be filled
with the damned, and after that 'forever shut'. Meanwhile the earth
will burn, and a new heaven and earth will arise from the ashes.
Eventually that too will pass, the Son will lay by his 'regal sceptre',
and 'God shall be all in all' (Book 3:341, quoted from I Corinthians
15:28).*

255. *maugre.* In spite of.

At God's command, the heavenly host adore the Son. Meanwhile
Satan lands on the outer shell of the created universe.

Here walked the fiend at large in spacious field.   430
As when a vulture on Imaus bred,
Whose snowy ridge the roving Tartar bounds,
Dislodging from a region scarce of prey
To gorge the flesh of lambs or yeanling kids
On hills where flocks are fed, flies toward the springs   435
Of Ganges or Hydaspes, Indian streams;
But in his way lights on the barren plains
Of Sericana, where Chineses drive
With sails and wind their cany wagons light:
So on this windy sea of land, the fiend   440
Walked up and down alone, bent on his prey;
Alone, for other creature in this place,
Living or lifeless, to be found was none.

From here, Satan can see that a retractable staircase stretches from
heaven's gate to the outer shell of the universe, where he stands. While
he watches:

The stairs were then let down, whether to dare

---

431. Imaus. Shown on sixteenth-century maps as a mountain range stretching north
from Afghanistan.   *432. bounds.* Is a barrier to.   *436. Hydaspes.* The Jhelum River in
the Punjab.   *438. Sericana.* In north-western China.   *439. cany wagons.* Land-yachts,
observed by early European travellers in China.

The fiend by easy ascent, or aggravate
His sad exclusion from the doors of bliss. 525

This is sometimes read as God taunting Satan. But it may be an offer of redemption. Satan has only to climb the stairs, submit, and beg forgiveness, to be saved. It is true that God knows he will not, but he has free will so in theory he could. On this reading, exclusion from heaven is his own choice, and knowledge that it is so may be what aggravates his bitterness.

He ignores the stairs, but looks down at the created universe through an aperture in its outer shell, and envies its beauty. Swooping down through the stars, he lands briefly on the sun, where an archangel, Uriel, is stationed. Having quickly disguised himself as a 'stripling cherub', Satan asks Uriel the way, and the unsuspecting archangel directs him to the Garden of Eden. Reaching earth, Satan lands on the top of Mount Niphates in Armenia.

BOOK 4

Though Satan has escaped from hell to earth, he feels, Milton tells us,
not joy but horror and despair. Wherever he goes, he carries hell within
him. Now that he is alone he is smitten by conscience. He is tormented,
too, by memory of his former state in heaven, and by thought of the
'worse sufferings' that, he realises, his misdeeds on earth will incur.
    Solitary on the mountain summit, he addresses the sun.

O thou that with surpassing glory crowned,
Lookst from thy sole dominion like the God
Of this new world; at whose sight all the stars
Hide their diminished heads; to thee I call,   35
But with no friendly voice, and add thy name,
O sun, to tell thee how I hate thy beams
That bring to my remembrance from what state
I fell, how glorious once above thy sphere;
Till pride and worse ambition threw me down,   40
Warring in heaven against heaven's matchless king:
Ah wherefore! He deserved no such return
From me, whom he created what I was

---

43. whom he created. Contradicting Satan's claim that angels created themselves (see
Book 5: 860).

In that bright eminence, and with his good
Upbraided none; nor was his service hard.   45
What could be less than to afford him praise,
The easiest recompense, and pay him thanks,
How due! Yet all his good proved ill in me,
And wrought but malice; lifted up so high
I sdeigned subjection, and thought one step higher   50
Would set me highest, and in a moment quit
The debt immense of endless gratitude,
So burdensome, still paying, still to owe;
Forgetful what from him I still received,
And understood not that a grateful mind   55
By owing owes not, but still pays, at once
Indebted and discharged; what burden then?
Oh had his powerful destiny ordained
Me some inferior angel, I had stood
Then happy; no unbounded hope had raised   60
Ambition. Yet why not? Some other power
As great might have aspired, and me, though mean,
Drawn to his part; but other powers as great
Fell not, but stand unshaken, from within
Or from without, to all temptations armed.   65
Hadst thou the same free will and power to stand?
Thou hadst: whom hast thou then or what to accuse,
But heaven's free love dealt equally to all?

50. sdeigned. Disdained.

Be then his love accursed, since love or hate,
To me alike, it deals eternal woe.   70
Nay cursed be thou; since against his thy will
Chose freely what it now so justly rues.
Me miserable! Which way shall I fly
Infinite wrath, and infinite despair?
Which way I fly is hell; myself am hell;   75
And in the lowest deep a lower deep
Still threatening to devour me opens wide,
To which the hell I suffer seems a heaven.
Oh then at last relent: Is there no place
Left for repentance, none for pardon left?   80
None left but by submission; and that word
Disdain forbids me, and my dread of shame
Among the spirits beneath, whom I seduced
With other promises and other vaunts
Than to submit, boasting I could subdue   85
The omnipotent. Ay me, they little know
How dearly I abide that boast so vain,
Under what torments inwardly I groan,
While they adore me on the throne of hell,
With diadem and sceptre high advanced   90
The lower still I fall, only supreme
In misery: such joy ambition finds.
But say I could repent and could obtain

87. *abide.* Suffer for.

By act of grace my former state; how soon
Would height recall high thoughts, how soon unsay   95
What feigned submission swore; ease would recant
Vows made in pain, as violent and void.
For never can true reconcilement grow
Where wounds of deadly hate have pierced so deep:
Which would but lead me to a worse relapse   100
And heavier fall: so should I purchase dear
Short intermission bought with double smart.
This knows my punisher; therefore as far
From granting he, as I from begging peace;
All hope excluded thus, behold, instead   105
Of us outcast, exiled, his new delight,
Mankind created, and for him this world.
So farewell hope, and with hope farewell fear,
Farewell remorse; all good to me is lost;
Evil be thou my good; by thee at least   110
Divided empire with heaven's king I hold,
By thee, and more than half perhaps will reign;
As man ere long, and this new world shall know.

Satan's fierce passions distort his face and Uriel, watching from far off on the sun, and seeing his 'mad demeanour', realises that he is an evil spirit. Satan, unaware that his disguise has been pierced, approaches the wall of Paradise.

110. by thee. By evil.

... now purer air
Meets his approach, and to the heart inspires
Vernal delight and joy, able to drive   155
All sadness but despair: now gentle gales,
Fanning their odoriferous wings dispense
Native perfumes, and whisper whence they stole
Those balmy spoils. As when to them who sail
Beyond the Cape of Hope, and now are past   160
Mozambic, off at sea north-east winds blow
Sabean odours from the spicy shore
Of Araby the blest, with such delay
Well pleased they slack their course, and many a league
Cheered with the grateful smell old Ocean smiles.   165
So entertained those odorous sweets the fiend.

*Satan leaps over the wall of Paradise with contemptuous ease, and
finds himself in the garden, which Milton describes.*

*For some critics the classical allusions he includes are a flaw, dimin-
ishing Paradise's naturalness. Others argue that for Milton's original
readers knowledge of the classics would be second nature.*

A happy rural seat of various view;
Groves whose rich trees wept odorous gums and balm,

161–4. The trade route up the African coast passed Mozambique (*Mozambic*) on the
way to the Arabian peninsula (*Araby*) and the biblical kingdom of Sheba. *Sabean.* Of
Sheba. *165. Ocean.* Oceanus, classical sea-god.

Others whose fruit burnished with golden rind
Hung amiable, Hesperian fables true,   250
If true, here only, and of delicious taste:
Betwixt them lawns, or level downs, and flocks
Grazing the tender herb, were interposed,
Or palmy hillock, or the flowery lap
Of some irriguous valley spread her store,   255
Flowers of all hue, and without thorn the rose:
Another side, umbrageous grots and caves
Of cool recess, o'er which the mantling vine
Lays forth her purple grape, and gently creeps
Luxuriant; meanwhile murmuring waters fall   260
Down the slope hills, dispersed, or in a lake,
That to the fringed bank with myrtle crowned
Her crystal mirror holds, unite their streams.
The birds their choir apply; airs, vernal airs,
Breathing the smell of field and grove, attune   265
The trembling leaves, while universal Pan
Knit with the Graces and the Hours in dance
Led on the eternal spring. Not that fair field
Of Enna, where Proserpin gathering flowers,

250. *amiable*. Desirable. *Hesperian*. Relating to the mythical Hesperides, who guarded golden apples in their island gardens. 255. *irriguous*. Well-watered. 257. *umbrageous grots*. Shady grottoes. 266–7. The nature-god *Pan* and the dancing *Graces* and *Hours* (or Seasons) feature in classical pastoral. 269–71. In myth the goddess Proserpina was seized from *Enna*, in Sicily, by *Dis*, god of the underworld, and sought by her mother *Ceres*.

Herself a fairer flower by gloomy Dis   270
Was gathered, which cost Ceres all that pain
To seek her through the world; nor that sweet grove
Of Daphne by Orontes, and the inspired
Castalian spring, might with this Paradise
Of Eden strive; nor that Nyseian isle   275
Girt with the river Triton, where old Cham,
Whom Gentiles Ammon call and Libyan Jove,
Hid Amalthea and her florid son,
Young Bacchus, from his stepdame Rhea's eye;
Nor where Abassin kings their issue guard,   280
Mount Amara, though this by some supposed
True Paradise under the Ethiop line
By Nilus' head, enclosed with shining rock,
A whole day's journey high, but wide remote
From this Assyrian garden, where the fiend   285
Saw undelighted all delight, all kind
Of living creatures new to sight and strange;
Two of far nobler shape erect and tall,
Godlike erect, with native honour clad

273–4. The grove of *Daphne* by the river *Orontes* had an oracle sacred to Apollo and
a spring named after the *Castalian* spring at Delphi.   275–9. *Ammon*, king of Libya,
was sometimes identified with Jupiter (*Jove*) or Noah's son Ham (*Cham*). He fathered
Bacchus and hid the child and his mother *Amalthea* from his wife *Rhea* on the island
of *Nysa*.   280–5. Emperors of Abyssinia were believed to seclude their sons among
gardens and palaces atop *Mount Amara*, south of the equator (*Ethiop line*) near the
source of the Nile (*Nilus*).

In naked majesty seemed lords of all,   290
And worthy seemed, for in their looks divine
The image of their glorious maker shone,
Truth, wisdom, sanctitude severe and pure,
Severe, but in true filial freedom placed;
Whence true authority in men; though both   295
Not equal, as their sex not equal seemed;
For contemplation he and valour formed;
For softness she and sweet attractive grace;
He for God only, she for God in him:
His fair large front and eye sublime declared   300
Absolute rule; and hyacinthine locks
Round from his parted forelock manly hung
Clustering, but not beneath his shoulders broad:
She as a veil down to the slender waist
Her unadorned golden tresses wore   305
Dishevelled, but in wanton ringlets waved
As the vine curls her tendrils, which implied
Subjection, but required with gentle sway,
And by her yielded, by him best received,
Yielded with coy submission, modest pride,   310
And sweet reluctant amorous delay.
Nor those mysterious parts were then concealed,

295. Whence. i.e. from God's image. *300. front.* Forehead. *301. hyacinthine.* Like
a hyacinth, perhaps in brightness of colour. Homer compares Odysseus' hair to a
hyacinth in the *Odyssey.*

Then was not guilty shame, dishonest shame
Of nature's works, honour dishonourable,
Sin-bred, how have ye troubled all mankind   315
With shows instead, mere shows of seeming pure,
And banished from man's life his happiest life,
Simplicity and spotless innocence.
So passed they naked on, nor shunned the sight
Of God or angel; for they thought no ill: 320
So hand in hand they passed, the loveliest pair,
That ever since in love's embraces met,
Adam the goodliest man of men since born
His sons, the fairest of her daughters Eve.
Under a tuft of shade that on a green   325
Stood whispering soft, by a fresh fountain side
They sat them down, and, after no more toil
Of their sweet gardening labour than sufficed
To recommend cool Zephyr, and made ease
More easy, wholesome thirst and appetite   330
More grateful, to their supper fruits they fell,
Nectarine fruits which the compliant boughs
Yielded them, sidelong as they sat recline
On the soft downy bank damasked with flowers;
The savoury pulp they chew, and in the rind,   335
Still as they thirsted, scoop the brimming stream;

329. *Zephyr.* The west wind.   332. *Nectarine.* Sweet as nectar.

Nor gentle purpose, nor endearing smiles
Wanted, nor youthful dalliance as beseems
Fair couple, linked in happy nuptial league,
Alone as they. About them frisking played   340
All beasts of the earth, since wild, and of all chase
In wood or wilderness, forest or den;
Sporting the lion ramped, and in his paw
Dandled the kid; bears, tigers, ounces, pards,
Gambolled before them, the unwieldy elephant,   345
To make them mirth used all his might, and wreathed
His lithe proboscis; close the serpent sly,
Insinuating, wove with Gordian twine
His braided train, and of his fatal guile
Gave proof unheeded; others on the grass   350
Couched, and now filled with pasture gazing sat,
Or bedward ruminating; for the sun
Declined was hasting now with prone career
To the Ocean Isles, and in the ascending scale
Of heaven the stars that usher evening rose;   355
When Satan still in gaze, as first he stood,
Scarce thus at length failed speech recovered sad.
     O hell! What do mine eyes with grief behold,
Into our room of bliss thus high advanced

338. Wanted. Were lacking. *beseems.* Befits. *344. ounces.* Lynxes. *pards.* Leopards.
347. proboscis. Trunk. *348. Gordian.* Like the legendary knot that could not be untied.
354. Ocean Isles. The Azores.

Creatures of other mould, earth-born perhaps,   360
Not spirits, yet to heavenly spirits bright
Little inferior; whom my thoughts pursue
With wonder, and could love, so lively shines
In them divine resemblance, and such grace
The hand that formed them on their shape hath poured.   365
Ah gentle pair, ye little think how nigh
Your change approaches, when all these delights
Will vanish and deliver ye to woe;
More woe, the more your taste is now of joy;
Happy, but for so happy ill secured   370
Long to continue, and this high seat your heaven
Ill fenced for heaven to keep out such a foe
As now is entered; yet no purposed foe
To you whom I could pity thus forlorn
Though I unpitied: league with you I seek,   375
And mutual amity so strait, so close,
That I with you must dwell, or you with me
Henceforth; my dwelling haply may not please
Like this fair Paradise, your sense, yet such
Accept your maker's work; he gave it me,   380
Which I as freely give; hell shall unfold,
To entertain you two, her widest gates,
And send forth all her kings; there will be room,
Not like these narrow limits, to receive
Your numerous offspring; if no better place,   385
Thank him who puts me, loath to this revenge,

On you who wrong me not, for him who wronged.
And should I at your harmless innocence
Melt, as I do, yet public reason just,
Honour and empire, with revenge enlarged,   390
By conquering this new world, compels me now
To do what else though damned I should abhor.
   So spoke the fiend, and with necessity,
The tyrant's plea, excused his devilish deeds.

*Satan continues to spy on Adam and Eve, disguising himself as vari-
ous animals, and overhears Adam speaking to Eve of their happiness, and of the one tree that bears fruit they must not eat on pain
of death ('whate'er death is,/Some dreadful thing no doubt', as Adam
light-heartedly puts it). Eve also rejoices in her happiness, and tells
Adam what she remembers about the day she was created.*

That day I oft remember, when from sleep
I first awaked, and found myself reposed   450
Under a shade on flowers, much wondering where
And what I was, whence thither brought, and how.
Not distant far from thence a murmuring sound
Of waters issued from a cave, and spread
Into a liquid plain, then stood unmoved   455
Pure as the expanse of heaven; I thither went
With unexperienced thought, and laid me down

387. for. In place of.

[82]

On the green bank, to look into the clear
Smooth lake, that to me seemed another sky.
As I bent down to look, just opposite   460
A shape within the watery gleam appeared
Bending to look on me, I started back,
It started back, but pleased I soon returned,
Pleased it returned as soon with answering looks
Of sympathy and love: there I had fixed   465
Mine eyes till now, and pined with vain desire,
Had not a voice thus warned me, What thou seest,
What there thou seest fair creature is thyself,
With thee it came and goes: but follow me,
And I will bring thee where no shadow stays   470
Thy coming, and thy soft embraces, he
Whose image thou art; him thou shalt enjoy
Inseparably thine, to him shalt bear
Multitudes like thyself, and thence be called
Mother of human race. What could I do,   475
But follow straight, invisibly thus led?
Till I espied thee, fair indeed and tall,
Under a platan, yet methought less fair,
Less winning soft, less amiably mild,
Than that smooth watery image: back I turned,   480
Thou following criedst aloud, Return fair Eve,
Whom fly'st thou? Whom thou fly'st, of him thou art,

470. stays. Awaits.

His flesh, his bone; to give thee being I lent
Out of my side to thee, nearest my heart
Substantial life, to have thee by my side   485
Henceforth, an individual solace dear;
Part of my soul I seek thee, and thee claim
My other half. With that thy gentle hand
Seized mine, I yielded, and from that time see
How beauty is excelled by manly grace,   490
And wisdom, which alone is truly fair.
    So spake our general mother, and with eyes
Of conjugal attraction, unreproved,
And meek surrender, half embracing leaned
On our first father, half her swelling breast   495
Naked met his under the flowing gold
Of her loose tresses hid.

Filled with envy, Satan cannot bear to watch the lovers embrace any
longer, but turns aside 'with jealous leer malign'.

Sight hateful, sight tormenting! Thus these two,   505
Imparadised in one another's arms,
The happier Eden, shall enjoy their fill
Of bliss on bliss, while I to hell am thrust,
Where neither joy nor love, but fierce desire,
Among our other torments not the least,   510
Still unfulfilled, with pain of longing pines;
Yet let me not forget what I have gained

From their own mouths; all is not theirs, it seems:
One fatal tree there stands of knowledge called,
Forbidden them to taste: knowledge forbidden?   515
Suspicious, reasonless. Why should their Lord
Envy them that? Can it be sin to know,
Can it be death? And do they only stand
By ignorance, is that their happy state,
The proof of their obedience and their faith?   520
Oh fair foundation laid whereon to build
Their ruin! Hence I will excite their minds
With more desire to know, and to reject
Envious commands, invented with design
To keep them low, whom knowledge might exalt   525
Equal with gods: aspiring to be such,
They taste and die; what likelier can ensue?

Satan continues to prowl around the garden. Meanwhile Uriel slides down a sunbeam to the gate of Paradise and tells Gabriel, the chief of the angelic guards posted there, of his suspicion that an evil spirit has entered Eden. Gabriel promises to have the garden searched.

   Night falls, and Adam tells Eve it is time for rest, reminding her that they must be up early next morning to tend the garden, which requires their constant care.

To whom thus Eve with perfect beauty adorned.
My author and disposer, what thou bidst   635
Unargued I obey: so God ordains,

God is thy law, thou mine: to know no more
Is woman's happiest knowledge and her praise.
With thee conversing I forget all time,
All seasons and their change, all please alike.   640
Sweet is the breath of morn, her rising sweet,
With charm of earliest birds: pleasant the sun
When first on this delightful land he spreads
His orient beams, on herb, tree, fruit, and flower,
Glistering with dew; fragrant the fertile earth   645
After soft showers; and sweet the coming on
Of grateful evening mild, then silent night,
With this her solemn bird and this fair moon,
And these the gems of heaven, her starry train:
But neither breath of morn when she ascends   650
With charm of earliest birds, nor rising sun
On this delightful land, nor herb, fruit, flower,
Glistering with dew, nor fragrance after showers,
Nor grateful evening mild, nor silent night
With this her solemn bird, nor walk by moon,   655
Or glittering starlight without thee is sweet.

*Eve goes on to ask Adam why the stars continue to shine at night, when
all creatures are asleep. He explains that mankind and animals are
only a part of God's creation.*

642. *charm.* Song.   647. *grateful.* Welcome.

Millions of spiritual creatures walk the earth
Unseen, both when we wake, and when we sleep:
All these with ceaseless praise his works behold
Both day and night: how often from the steep   680
Of echoing hill or thicket have we heard
Celestial voices to the midnight air,
Sole, or responsive each to other's note
Singing their great creator: oft in bands
While they keep watch, or nightly rounding walk   685
With heavenly touch of instrumental sounds
In full harmonic number joined, their songs
Divide the night, and lift our thoughts to heaven.
   Thus talking hand in hand alone they passed
On to their blissful bower; it was a place   690
Chosen by the sovereign planter, when he framed
All things to man's delightful use; the roof
Of thickest covert was inwoven shade
Laurel and myrtle, and what higher grew
Of firm and fragrant leaf; on either side   695
Acanthus, and each odorous bushy shrub
Fenced up the verdant wall; each beauteous flower,
Iris all hues, roses, and jessamin,
Reared high their flourished heads between, and wrought
Mosaic; underfoot the violet,   700
Crocus, and hyacinth with rich inlay

698. jessamin. Jasmine.

Broidered the ground, more coloured than with stone
Of costliest emblem: other creature here,
Beast, bird, insect, or worm durst enter none,
Such was their awe of man. In shadier bower   705
More sacred and sequestered, though but feigned,
Pan or Silvanus never slept, nor nymph,
Nor Faunus haunted. Here in close recess
With flowers, garlands, and sweet-smelling herbs
Espoused Eve decked first her nuptial bed;   710
And heavenly choirs the hymenean sung,
What day the genial angel to our sire
Brought her in naked beauty more adorned,
More lovely than Pandora, whom the gods
Endowed with all their gifts, and oh too like   715
In sad event, when to the unwiser son
Of Japhet brought by Hermes, she ensnared
Mankind with her fair looks, to be avenged
On him who had stole Jove's authentic fire.

   Thus at their shady lodge arrived, both stood,   720
Both turned, and under open sky adored
The God that made both sky, air, earth, and heaven
Which they beheld, the moon's resplendent globe

707–8. *Pan, Sylvanus* and *Faunus* were woodland gods from classical pastoral. *711.*
hymenean. Wedding hymn. *712. genial.* Related to generation. *714–19.* In the myth
Zeus (*Jove*), angry at the theft of fire by Prometheus, son of *Japhet*, creates the first
woman, *Pandora*, and sends her, with a closed casket, to Prometheus, which his
unwiser brother Epimetheus opens, filling the earth with diseases and calamities.

And starry pole: Thou also mad'st the night,
Maker omnipotent, and thou the day,   725
Which we, in our appointed work employed
Have finished happy in our mutual help
And mutual love, the crown of all our bliss
Ordained by thee, and this delicious place
For us too large, where thy abundance wants   730
Partakers, and uncropped falls to the ground.
But thou hast promised from us two a race
To fill the earth, who shall with us extol
Thy goodness infinite, both when we wake,
And when we seek, as now, thy gift of sleep.   735
    This said unanimous, and other rites
Observing none, but adoration pure
Which God likes best, into their inmost bower
Handed they went; and eased the putting off
These troublesome disguises which we wear.   740

*Milton does not describe Adam and Eve's love-making, having already
associated voyeurism with Satan. Instead, after what seems to be an
unfortunate attempt at mannish jocularity ('nor turned I ween/Adam
from his fair spouse'), he praises wedded love and deplores its alternatives such as 'adulterous lust', 'harlots' and 'court amours'. He returns to
Adam and Eve only when their love-making is over.*

740. *disguises.* Clothes.

These lulled by nightingales embracing slept,
And on their naked limbs the flowery roof
Showered roses, which the morn repaired. Sleep on
Blest pair; and O yet happiest if ye seek
No happier state, and know to know no more.   775

*Meanwhile Gabriel orders his angelic guards to search the garden and
two of them, Ithuriel and Zephon, find Satan, disguised as a toad,
squatting by Eve's ear and trying to insinuate evil thoughts into her
mind while she sleeps.*

Him thus intent Ithuriel with his spear   810
Touched lightly, for no falsehood can endure
Touch of celestial temper, but returns
Of force to its own likeness: up he starts
Discovered and surprised. As when a spark
Lights on a heap of nitrous powder, laid   815
Fit for the tun some magazine to store
Against a rumoured war, the smutty grain
With sudden blaze diffused, inflames the air;
So started up in his own shape the fiend.
Back stepped those two fair angels, half amazed   820
So sudden to behold the grisly king;
Yet thus, unmoved with fear, accost him soon.
    Which of those rebel spirits adjudged to hell

815. nitrous powder. Gunpowder.   *816. tun.* Barrel.

Com'st thou, escaped thy prison, and transformed,
Why satst thou like an enemy in wait,   825
Here watching at the head of these that sleep?
    Know ye not then, said Satan, filled with scorn,
Know ye not me? Ye knew me once no mate
For you, there sitting where ye durst not soar:
Not to know me argues yourselves unknown,   830
The lowest of your throng; or, if ye know,
Why ask ye, and superfluous begin
Your message, like to end as much in vain?
To whom thus Zephon, answering scorn with scorn.
    Think not, revolted spirit, thy shape the same,   835
Or undiminished brightness, to be known,
As when thou stood'st in heaven upright and pure;
That glory then, when thou no more wast good,
Departed from thee; and thou resemblest now
Thy sin and place of doom obscure and foul.   840
But come, for thou, be sure, shalt give account
To him who sent us, whose charge is to keep
This place inviolable, and these from harm.
    So spake the cherub; and his grave rebuke,
Severe in youthful beauty, added grace   845
Invincible: abashed the devil stood,
And felt how awful goodness is, and saw
Virtue in her shape how lovely; saw, and pined

830. Not . . . unknown. If you don't know who I am you must be nobodies.

[91]

His loss; but chiefly to find here observed
His lustre visibly impaired; yet seemed   850
Undaunted.

The two angelic guards take Satan to where Gabriel and the other
guards are waiting. Gabriel questions him and he answers with scorn
and defiance. It looks as if there will be a fight. But God, to prevent
any damage to Paradise, hangs out his 'golden scales' (the constella-
tion Libra) in heaven. They show that more will be lost than gained
through fighting, and Satan takes this to mean that he will lose.

The fiend looked up, and knew
His mounted scale aloft; nor more; but fled
Murmuring, and with him fled the shades of night.   1015

BOOK 5

Adam wakes to find that Eve is still asleep, and is looking flushed and disturbed. He wakes her gently, and she tells him she has had a bad dream (the result, though she and Adam do not know it, of Satan putting thoughts into her mind when he squatted by her ear as a toad).

       ... methought   35
Close at mine ear one called me forth to walk
With gentle voice, I thought it thine; it said,
   Why sleepst thou Eve? Now is the pleasant time,
The cool, the silent, save where silence yields
To the night-warbling bird, that now awake   40
Tunes sweetest his love-laboured song; now reigns
Full-orbed the moon, and with more pleasing light
Shadowy sets off the face of things; in vain,
If none regard; heaven wakes with all his eyes,
Whom to behold but thee, nature's desire,   45
In whose sight all things joy, with ravishment
Attracted by thy beauty still to gaze.
   I rose as at thy call, but found thee not;
To find thee I directed then my walk;

40. bird. Nightingale. *48. thy.* Adam's.

And on, methought, alone I passed through ways   50
That brought me on a sudden to the tree
Of interdicted knowledge: fair it seemed,
Much fairer to my fancy than by day:
And as I wondering looked, beside it stood
One shaped and winged like one of those from heaven   55
By us oft seen; his dewy locks distilled
Ambrosia; on that tree he also gazed;
And O fair plant, said he, with fruit surcharged,
Deigns none to ease thy load and taste thy sweet,
Nor god, nor man; is knowledge so despised?   60
Or envy, or what reserve forbids to taste?
Forbid who will, none shall from me withhold
Longer thy offered good, why else set here?
This said he paused not, but with venturous arm
He plucked, he tasted; me damp horror chilled   65
At such bold words vouched with a deed so bold:
But he thus overjoyed: O fruit divine,
Sweet of thyself, but much more sweet thus cropped,
Forbidden here, it seems, as only fit
For gods, yet able to make gods of men: 70
And why not gods of men, since good, the more
Communicated, more abundant grows,
The author not impaired, but honoured more?

---

52. interdicted. Forbidden. *61. Or . . . forbids.* Or [does] envy or some restriction [on God's part] forbid? *66. vouched.* Confirmed.

Here, happy creature, fair angelic Eve,
Partake thou also; happy though thou art,   75
Happier thou mayst be, worthier canst not be:
Taste this, and be henceforth among the gods,
Thyself a goddess, not to earth confined,
But sometimes in the air, as we, sometimes
Ascend to heaven, by merit thine, and see   80
What life the gods live there, and such live thou.
   So saying, he drew nigh, and to me held,
Even to my mouth of that same fruit held part
Which he had plucked; the pleasant savoury smell
So quickened appetite, that I, methought,   85
Could not but taste. Forthwith up to the clouds
With him I flew, and underneath beheld
The earth outstretched immense, a prospect wide
And various: wondering at my flight and change
To this high exaltation. Suddenly   90
My guide was gone, and I, methought, sunk down,
And fell asleep; but oh how glad I waked
To find this but a dream!

*Critics are divided over whether Eve's dream makes her more likely to
fall (because in the dream the fruit makes her feel like an angel) or less
likely (because the dream horrifies her and should act as a warning).*

   *Adam comforts her, and delivers a brief lecture about dreams and
human intellectual faculties. He also tells her, surprisingly, that:*

[95]

Evil into the mind of god or man
May come and go, so unapproved, and leave
No spot of blame behind: which gives me hope
That what in sleep thou didst abhor to dream,   120
Waking thou never wilt consent to do.

*By 'god' Adam may mean 'angel' (see Book 1:629, note) – or he may
realise that God's omniscience must extend to evil.*

*Eve is comforted and he kisses away her tears. They raise their voices
in a spontaneous hymn of praise to God, before setting off for a day's
gardening.*

*God, looking down from heaven, watches them 'with pity'. He sum-
mons the archangel Raphael and instructs him to fly down to earth
and warn Adam that an enemy is at large in the garden, plotting
to bring about man's fall through deceit and lies. Since God knows
that Adam will fall, this precaution might seem futile. But God issues
his warning, he explains, to put himself in the clear. Adam, though
'wilfully transgressing', will not be able to 'pretend' that he did so
'unforewarned'.*

*Raphael must also know that Adam will fall, having been present
with the heavenly host when God predicted it (Book 3:95). However,
he flies down through the heavenly spheres to deliver his warning:*

                    . . . and now is come
Into the blissful field, through groves of myrrh,
And flowering odours, cassia, nard, and balm;
A wilderness of sweets; for nature here

Wantoned as in her prime, and played at will   295
Her virgin fancies, pouring forth more sweet,
Wild above rule or art, enormous bliss.
Him through the spicy forest onward come
Adam discerned, as in the door he sat
Of his cool bower, while now the mounted sun   300
Shot down direct his fervid rays to warm
Earth's inmost womb, more warmth than Adam needs:
And Eve within, due at her hour prepared
For dinner savoury fruits, of taste to please
True appetite, and not disrelish thirst   305
Of nectareous draughts between, from milky stream,
Berry or grape.

*Adam strides out to meet his heavenly guest, and his naked perfection
is:*

More solemn than the tedious pomp that waits
On princes, when their rich retinue long   355
Of horses led, and grooms besmeared with gold,
Dazzles the crowd, and sets them all agape.

*Raphael joins Adam and Eve at dinner, and Adam worries that their
earthly food – fruit, berries, kernels and grains – may not be suitable*

298–9. Him . . . Adam. Inversion. Normal word order would be 'Adam discerned him'.
304. savoury. Appetising. *306. nectareous.* Like nectar.

for angels. Raphael reassures him that angels, like all creatures, need food. Their angelic digestion refines matter into spirit, and this illustrates, he goes on to explain, a universal principle. If Adam and Eve remain obedient, he speculates, they too may be refined from matter to spirit.

O Adam, one almighty is, from whom
All things proceed, and up to him return,   470
If not depraved from good, created all
Such to perfection, one first matter all,
Indued with various forms, various degrees
Of substance, and in things that live, of life;
But more refined, more spirituous and pure,   475
As nearer to him placed, or nearer tending,
Each in their several active spheres assigned,
Till body up to spirit work, in bounds
Proportioned to each kind. So from the root
Springs lighter the green stalk, from thence the leaves   480
More airy, last the bright consummate flower
Spirits odorous breathes: flowers and their fruit
Man's nourishment, by gradual scale sublimed,
To vital spirits aspire, to animal,
To intellectual, give both life and sense,   485
Fancy and understanding, whence the soul

484–5. vital spirits. Believed in seventeenth-century medicine to flow from the blood: *animal* spirits gave sensation and movement; *intellectual* spirits, the higher faculties.

Reason receives, and reason is her being,
Discursive, or intuitive; discourse
Is oftest yours, the latter most is ours,
Differing but in degree, of kind the same.   490
Wonder not then, what God for you saw good
If I refuse not, but convert, as you
To proper substance; time may come when men
With angels may participate, and find
No inconvenient diet, nor too light fare;   495
And from these corporal nutriments perhaps
Your bodies may at last turn all to spirit,
Improved by tract of time, and, winged, ascend
Ethereal, as we, or may at choice
Here or in heavenly paradises dwell;   500
If ye be found obedient, and retain
Unalterably firm his love entire
Whose progeny you are. Meanwhile enjoy
Your fill what happiness this happy state
Can comprehend, incapable of more.   505

Noting Raphael's caution about obedience, Adam asks how any
creature could possibly disobey God. Raphael replies that even angels
have done so, and have fallen: all creatures have free will. Adam

488–9. Raphael distinguishes between human discursive reason, which works through
deduction, and angelic intuitive reason, which is immediate. *491–2. Wonder . . . refuse*
not. Do not be surprised if I don't refuse the food God considered good for you.

begs Raphael to tell him how the angels fell, and Raphael says he
will try, but it is difficult, because human understanding is limited.
However:

     . . . what surmounts the reach
Of human sense, I shall delineate so,
By likening spiritual to corporal forms,
As may express them best, though what if earth
Be but a shadow of heaven, and things therein   575
Each to other like, more than on earth is thought?
   As yet this world was not, and Chaos wild
Reigned where these heavens now roll, where earth now rests
Upon her centre poised, when on a day
(For time, though in eternity, applied   580
To motion, measures all things durable
By present, past, and future), on such day
As heaven's great year brings forth, the empyreal host
Of angels, by imperial summons called,
Innumerable before the almighty's throne   585
Forthwith from all the ends of heaven, appeared
Under their hierarchs in orders bright;
Ten thousand thousand ensigns high advanced,
Standards and gonfalons twixt van and rear
Stream in the air, and for distinction serve   590
Of hierarchies, of orders, and degrees;

587. hierarchs. Leaders. *589. gonfalons.* Banners.

Or in their glittering tissues bear imblazed
Holy memorials, acts of zeal and love
Recorded eminent. Thus when in orbs
Of circuit inexpressible they stood,   595
Orb within orb, the Father infinite,
By whom in bliss embosomed sat the Son,
Amidst as from a flaming mount, whose top
Brightness had made invisible, thus spake.
    Hear all ye angels, progeny of light,   600
Thrones, dominations, princedoms, virtues, powers,
Hear my decree, which unrevoked shall stand.
This day I have begot whom I declare
My only Son, and on this holy hill
Him have anointed, whom ye now behold   605
At my right hand; your head I him appoint;
And by myself have sworn to him shall bow
All knees in heaven, and shall confess him Lord:
Under his great vicegerent reign abide
United as one individual soul,   610
For ever happy; him who disobeys
Me disobeys, breaks union, and that day
Cast out from God and blessed vision, falls

592. imblazed. Emblazoned. *601.* Renaissance authorities identified nine ranks of
angel in three descending orders: seraphim, cherubim, thrones; dominions, virtues,
powers; principalities, archangels, angels. *603–4.* From Psalm 2:7, 'Thou art my Son:
this day have I begotten thee'. *609. Vicegerent reign.* Delegated rule. Milton believed
the Son was subordinate to the Father and received all his powers from him.

Into utter darkness, deep engulfed, his place
Ordained without redemption, without end.   615

*The heavenly host, Raphael relates, all seemed pleased by God's an-
nouncement. But some were not. When night fell:*

     . . . the angelic throng,   650
Dispersed in bands and files, their camp extend
By living streams among the trees of life,
Pavilions numberless, and sudden reared,
Celestial tabernacles, where they slept
Fanned with cool winds, save those who, in their course,   655
Melodious hymns about the sovereign throne
Alternate all night long: but not so waked
Satan, so call him now, his former name
Is heard no more in heaven; he of the first,
If not the first archangel, great in power,   660
In favour and pre-eminence, yet fraught
With envy against the Son of God, that day
Honoured by his great Father, and proclaimed
Messiah king anointed, could not bear
Through pride that sight, and thought himself impaired.   665
Deep malice thence conceiving and disdain,
Soon as midnight brought on the dusky hour

658. *his former name.* Sometimes given, following Isaiah 14:12–15, as Lucifer, the name
Raphael uses at line 760.

Friendliest to sleep and silence, he resolved
With all his legions to dislodge, and leave
Unworshipped, unobeyed the throne supreme,   670
Contemptuous, and his next subordinate
Awak'ning, thus to him in secret spake.
   Sleepst thou companion dear, what sleep can close
Thy eyelids? And rememberest what decree
Of yesterday, so late hath passed the lips   675
Of heaven's almighty? Thou to me thy thoughts
Wast wont, I mine to thee was wont to impart;
Both waking we were one; how then can now
Thy sleep dissent? New laws thou seest imposed;
New laws from him who reigns, new minds may raise   680
In us who serve, new counsels, to debate
What doubtful may ensue, more in this place
To utter is not safe. Assemble thou
Of all those myriads which we lead the chief;
Tell them that by command, ere yet dim night   685
Her shadowy cloud withdraws, I am to haste,
And all who under me their banners wave,
Homeward with flying march where we possess
The quarters of the north, there to prepare
Fit entertainment to receive our king   690
The great Messiah, and his new commands,

---

671. his next subordinate. Raphael avoids giving his heavenly name. Beelzebub is his
fallen name.

Who speedily through all the hierarchies
Intends to pass triumphant, and give laws.
   So spake the false archangel, and infused
Bad influence into the unwary breast   695
Of his associate; he together calls,
Or several one by one, the regent powers,
Under him regent, tells, as he was taught,
That the most high commanding, now ere night,
Now ere dim night had disencumbered heaven,   700
The great hierarchal standard was to move;
Tells the suggested cause, and casts between
Ambiguous words and jealousies, to sound
Or taint integrity; but all obeyed
The wonted signal, and superior voice   705
Of their great potentate; for great indeed
His name, and high was his degree in heaven;
His countenance, as the morning star that guides
The starry flock, allured them, and with lies
Drew after him the third part of heaven's host: 710
Meanwhile the eternal eye, whose sight discerns
Abstrusest thoughts, from forth his holy mount
And from within the golden lamps that burn
Nightly before him, saw, without their light,
Rebellion rising, saw in whom, how spread   715
Among the sons of morn, what multitudes

697. *regent.* Ruling.

Were banded to oppose his high decree;
And smiling to his only Son thus said.
   Son, thou in whom my glory I behold
In full resplendence, heir of all my might,   720
Nearly it now concerns us to be sure
Of our omnipotence, and with what arms
We mean to hold what anciently we claim
Of deity or empire; such a foe
Is rising, who intends to erect his throne   725
Equal to ours, throughout the spacious north;
Nor so content, hath in his thought to try
In battle, what our power is, or our right.
Let us advise, and to this hazard draw
With speed what force is left, and all employ   730
In our defence, lest unawares we lose
This our high place, our sanctuary, our hill.
   To whom the Son with calm aspect and clear
Lightning divine, ineffable, serene,
Made answer. Mighty Father, thou thy foes   735
Justly hast in derision, and secure
Laughst at their vain designs and tumults vain,
Matter to me of glory, whom their hate
Illustrates, when they see all regal power

---

718. smiling. Being omnipotent, God can joke about possible defeat. Critics have
found this insensitive. But the Father's 'derision' and scornful laughter were biblical
(Psalm 2:4). *739. Illustrates.* Makes glorious.

Given me to quell their pride, and in event 740
Know whether I be dextrous to subdue
Thy rebels, or be found the worst in heaven.
    So spake the Son, but Satan, with his powers,
Far was advanced on winged speed, an host
Innumerable as the stars of night, 745
Or stars of morning, dewdrops, which the sun
Impearls on every leaf and every flower.
Regions they passed, the mighty regencies
Of seraphim and potentates and thrones,
In their triple degrees, regions to which 750
All thy dominion, Adam, is no more
Than what this garden is to all the earth,
And all the sea, from one entire globose
Stretched into longitude; which having passed
At length into the limits of the north 755
They came, and Satan to his royal seat
High on a hill, far blazing, as a mount
Raised on a mount, with pyramids and towers
From diamond quarries hewn, and rocks of gold,
The palace of great Lucifer (so call 760
That structure in the dialect of men
Interpreted), which not long after, he

749–50. See Book 5:601 note. 753–4. *globose . . . longitude.* If the earth's sphere were
flattened out. 756. *They came, and Satan.* The verb 'came' applies to both 'They' and
'Satan'.

Affecting all equality with God,
In imitation of that mount whereon
Messiah was declared in sight of heaven,   765
The Mountain of the Congregation called;
For thither he assembled all his train,
Pretending so commanded to consult
About the great reception of their king,
Thither to come, and with calumnious art   770
Of counterfeited truth thus held their ears.
   Thrones, dominations, princedoms, virtues, powers,
If these magnific titles yet remain
Not merely titular, since by decree
Another now hath to himself engrossed   775
All power, and us eclipsed under the name
Of king anointed, for whom all this haste
Of midnight march, and hurried meeting here,
This only to consult how we may best
With what may be devised of honours new   780
Receive him coming to receive from us
Knee-tribute yet unpaid, prostration vile,
Too much to one, but double how endured,
To one and to his image now proclaimed?
But what if better counsels might erect   785
Our minds and teach us to cast off this yoke?

783. *double*. To both Father and Son.

Will ye submit your necks, and choose to bend
The supple knee? Ye will not, if I trust
To know ye right, or if ye know yourselves
Natives and sons of heaven possessed before   790
By none, and if not equal all, yet free,
Equally free, for orders and degrees
Jar not with liberty, but well consist.
Who can in reason then or right assume
Monarchy over such as live by right   795
His equals, if in power and splendour less,
In freedom equal? Or can introduce
Law and edict on us, who without law
Err not, much less for this to be our lord,
And look for adoration, to the abuse   800
Of those imperial titles which assert
Our being ordained to govern, not to serve?

 Thus far his bold discourse without control
Had audience; when among the seraphim
Abdiel, than whom none with more zeal adored   805
The deity, and divine commands obeyed,
Stood up, and in a flame of zeal severe
The current of his fury thus opposed.
 Oh argument blasphemous, false and proud!

795. *Monarchy.* Some critics see Satan's speech as reflecting Milton's fierce republicanism.
805. *Abdiel.* Means 'Servant of God'. There is no biblical basis for his lonely defiance,
which may reflect Milton's after the Restoration.

Words which no ear ever to hear in heaven   810
Expected, least of all from thee, ingrate,
In place thyself so high above thy peers.
Canst thou with impious obloquy condemn
The just decree of God, pronounced and sworn,
That to his only Son, by right endued   815
With regal sceptre, every soul in heaven
Shall bend the knee, and in that honour due
Confess him rightful king? Unjust, thou sayst,
Flatly unjust, to bind with laws the free,
And equal over equals to let reign,   820
One over all with unsucceeded power.
Shalt thou give law to God, shalt thou dispute
With him the points of liberty, who made
Thee what thou art, and formed the powers of heaven
Such as he pleased, and circumscribed their being?   825
Yet, by experience taught, we know how good,
And of our good, and of our dignity
How provident he is, how far from thought
To make us less, bent rather to exalt
Our happy state, under one head more near   830
United. But to grant it thee unjust,
That equal over equals monarch reign;
Thyself though great and glorious dost thou count,

811. *ingrate.* Ungrateful. 817. Echoing Philippians 2:10: 'at the name of Jesus every
knee should bow'. 821. *unsucceeded.* Never yielding to any successor.

[109]

Or all angelic nature joined in one,
Equal to him begotten Son? By whom   835
As by his word the mighty Father made
All things, even thee, and all the spirits of heaven
By him created in their bright degrees,
Crowned them with glory, and to their glory named
Thrones, dominations, princedoms, virtues, powers,   840
Essential powers, nor by his reign obscured,
But more illustrious made, since he the head
One of our number thus reduced becomes,
His laws our laws, all honour to him done
Returns our own. Cease then this impious rage,   845
And tempt not these; but hasten to appease
The incensed Father, and the incensed Son,
While pardon may be found in time besought.
    So spake the fervent angel; but his zeal
None seconded, as out of season judged,   850
Or singular and rash, whereat rejoiced
The apostate, and more haughty thus replied.
    That we were formed then sayst thou? And the work
Of secondary hands, by task transferred
From Father to his Son? Strange point and new!   855

835–7. Echoing Colossians 1.16: 'for by him [the Son] were all things created'. Milton writes in *Christian Doctrine* that God the Father created the world 'through' the Son. *843. reduced.* There seems no basis for Abdiel's belief that the Father's exaltation of the Son reduced him to angelic status. *852. The apostate.* Satan.

Doctrine which we would know whence learned: who saw
When this creation was? Rememberest thou
Thy making, while the maker gave thee being?
We know no time when we were not as now;
Know none before us, self-begot, self-raised   860
By our own quickening power, when fatal course
Had circled his full orb, the birth mature
Of this our native heaven, ethereal sons.
Our puissance is our own, our own right hand
Shall teach us highest deeds, by proof to try   865
Who is our equal; then thou shalt behold
Whether by supplication we intend
Address, and to begirt the almighty throne
Beseeching or besieging. This report,
These tidings carry to the anointed king;   870
And fly, ere evil intercept thy flight.

 　　He said, and as the sound of waters deep
Hoarse murmur echoed to his words applause
Through the infinite host, nor less for that
The flaming seraph fearless, though alone   875
Encompassed round with foes, thus answered bold.

 　　O alienate from God, O spirit accursed,
Forsaken of all good; I see thy fall
Determined, and thy hapless crew involved
In this perfidious fraud, contagion spread   880

---

861. quickening. Enlivening. *fatal.* Fated. *864. puissance.* Power.

Both of thy crime and punishment: henceforth
No more be troubled how to quit the yoke
Of God's Messiah; those indulgent laws
Will not be now vouchsafed, other decrees
Against thee are gone forth without recall;   885
That golden sceptre which thou didst reject
Is now an iron rod to bruise and break
Thy disobedience. Well thou didst advise,
Yet not for thy advice or threats I fly
These wicked tents devoted, lest the wrath   890
Impendent, raging into sudden flame,
Distinguish not: for soon expect to feel
His thunder on thy head, devouring fire.
Then who created thee lamenting learn,
When who can uncreate thee thou shalt know.   895
   So spake the seraph Abdiel, faithful found
Among the faithless, faithful only he;
Among innumerable false, unmoved,
Unshaken, unseduced, unterrified,
His loyalty he kept, his love, his zeal;   900
Nor number, nor example, with him wrought
To swerve from truth, or change his constant mind,
Though single. From amidst them forth he passed,

882. *quit*. Requite, respond to.   *887. iron rod*. Echoing Psalm 2:9: 'thou shalt break
them with a rod of iron'.   *890. devoted*. Given over to destruction.   *891. Impendent*.
Overhanging.   *892. Distinguish not*. Does not distinguish the innocent from the
guilty.

[112]

Long way through hostile scorn, which he sustained
Superior, nor of violence feared aught; 905
And with retorted scorn his back he turned
On those proud towers to swift destruction doomed.

906. *retorted*. Returned.

BOOK 6

Raphael continues his narrative of events in heaven before the evil angels fell. He tells how Abdiel flew back to the courts of heaven and found the good angels preparing for war. God's voice, issuing from a golden cloud, congratulated him on his loyalty, and then gave commands to the archangel Michael, the leader of the heavenly army.

Go Michael, of celestial armies prince,
And thou in military prowess next,   45
Gabriel, lead forth to battle these my sons
Invincible, lead forth my armed saints,
By thousands and by millions ranged for fight,
Equal in number to that godless crew
Rebellious, them with fire and hostile arms   50
Fearless assault, and to the brow of heaven
Pursuing, drive them out from God and bliss,
Into their place of punishment, the gulf
Of Tartarus, which ready opens wide
His fiery chaos to receive their fall.   55

Critics have pointed out that God does not give Michael all the

54. *Tartarus*. A depth beneath Hades in Greek myth.

available forces. Since Michael's army is one third of heaven's popula-
tion, and Satan's rebels account for another third, God evidently keeps
the remaining third in reserve for his Son to lead in eventual victory.
Being omniscient, God knows (as he later explains to the Son, lines
693–4 below) that Michael's army will not be able to drive the evil
angels out. Commanding them to do so is just a test of their obedience
(though, as with all God's tests, he knows the outcome beforehand).

Michael's and Satan's armies join battle and Satan and Michael
meet in single combat. Both are 'next to almighty':

. . . but the sword   320
Of Michael from the armoury of God
Was given him, tempered so that neither keen
Nor solid might resist that edge: it met
The sword of Satan with steep force to smite
Descending, and in half cut sheer, nor stayed,   325
But with swift wheel reverse, deep entering shared
All his right side; then Satan first knew pain,
And writhed him to and fro convolved; so sore
The griding sword with discontinuous wound
Passed through him, but the ethereal substance closed,   330
Not long divisible, and from the gash
A stream of nectarous humour issuing flowed
Sanguine, such as celestial spirits may bleed,

326. shared. Sheared. *329. griding.* Slicing and rasping. *332. nectarous.* Angels drink
nectar in heaven (Book 5:633) so they bleed something nectar-like.

And all his armour stained, erewhile so bright.
Forthwith on all sides to his aid was run   335
By angels many and strong, who interposed
Defence, while others bore him on their shields
Back to his chariot, where it stood retired
From off the files of war; there they him laid
Gnashing for anguish and despite and shame,   340
To find himself not matchless, and his pride
Humbled by such rebuke, so far beneath
His confidence to equal God in power.
Yet soon he healed; for spirits that live throughout
Vital in every part, not as frail man   345
In entrails, heart or head, liver or reins,
Cannot but by annihilating die;
Nor in their liquid texture mortal wound
Receive, no more than can the fluid air:
All heart they live, all head, all eye, all ear,   350
All intellect, all sense, and as they please,
They limb themselves, and colour, shape, or size
Assume, as likes them best, condense or rare.

*The first day's battle ends, with neither side gaining a decisive advan-
tage, and the armies separate at nightfall. During the night Satan
teaches his followers how to manufacture gunpowder and forge cannon*

335–6. *was run . . . By angels.* A Latin construction meaning 'angels ran to his aid'.
346. *reins.* Kidneys.   353. *condense or rare.* Solid or rarefied.

out of materials dug from heaven's substrata. When the second day's
battle begins the first volley of the devils' artillery causes havoc among
Michael's warriors.

       . . . down they fell
By thousands, angel on archangel rolled,
The sooner for their arms – unarmed, they might   595
Have easily as spirits evaded swift
By quick contraction or remove; but now
Foul dissipation followed and forced rout;
Nor served it to relax their serried files.
What should they do? If on they rushed, repulse   600
Repeated, and indecent overthrow
Doubled, would render them yet more despised,
And to their foes a laughter; for in view
Stood ranked of seraphim another row
In posture to displode their second tire   605
Of thunder: back defeated to return
They worse abhorred. Satan beheld their plight,
And to his mates thus in derision called.
   O friends, why come not on these victors proud?
Erewhile they fierce were coming, and when we,   610
To entertain them fair with open front
And breast, (what could we more?) propounded terms

598. dissipation. Dispersal. *605. displode.* Fire. *tire.* Volley. *611. open front.* Sarcastic
pun: (1) guileless face (2) extended front line.

[118]

Of composition, straight they changed their minds,
Flew off, and into strange vagaries fell,
As they would dance, yet for a dance they seemed   615
Somewhat extravagant and wild, perhaps
For joy of offered peace: but I suppose,
If our proposals once again were heard,
We should compel them to a quick result.
   To whom thus Belial in like gamesome mood.   620
Leader, the terms we sent were terms of weight,
Of hard contents, and full of force urged home,
Such as we might perceive amused them all,
And stumbled many; who receives them right,
Had need from head to foot well understand;   625
Not understood, this gift they have besides,
They show us when our foes walk not upright.
   So they among themselves in pleasant vein
Stood scoffing, heightened in their thoughts beyond
All doubt of victory, eternal might   630
To match with their inventions they presumed
So easy, and of his thunder made a scorn,
And all his host derided, while they stood
Awhile in trouble: but they stood not long,

---

621. terms of weight. (1) Treaty conditions (2) cannon balls. Belial imitates Satan's
sarcasm. *623. amused them.* (1) occupied their attention (2) entertained them. *625.*
understand. (1) prop up (2) comprehend. *627. walk not upright.* (1) are devious (2) lose
their footing.

Rage prompted them at length, and found them arms   635
Against such hellish mischief fit to oppose.
Forthwith (behold the excellence, the power
Which God hath in his mighty angels placed)
Their arms away they threw, and to the hills
(For earth hath this variety from heav'n   640
Of pleasure situate in hill and dale)
Light as the lightning glimpse they ran, they flew,
From their foundations loosening to and fro
They plucked the seated hills with all their load,
Rocks, waters, woods, and by the shaggy tops   645
Up lifting bore them in their hands: amaze,
Be sure, and terror seized the rebel host,
When coming towards them so dread they saw
The bottom of the mountains upward turned,
Till on those cursed engines' triple row   650
They saw them whelmed, and all their confidence
Under the weight of mountains buried deep.
Themselves invaded next, and on their heads
Main promontories flung, which in the air
Came shadowing, and oppressed whole legions armed,   655
Their armour helped their harm, crushed in and bruised
Into their substance pent, which wrought them pain
Implacable, and many a dolorous groan,

---

651. whelmed. Dropped so as to engulf. *656. helped.* Increased.   *657. their substance pent.* Their enclosed bodies.

Long struggling underneath, ere they could wind
Out of such prison, though spirits of purest light,   660
Purest at first, now gross by sinning grown.

The devils start to throw hills in retaliation and there is a danger that
heaven will be ruined. But God intervenes and, addressing his Son,
directs him to vanquish the devils and end the war.

. . . two days are past,
Two days, as we compute the days of heaven,   685
Since Michael and his powers went forth to tame
These disobedient; sore hath been their fight,
As likeliest was, when two such foes met armed;
For to themselves I left them; and thou knowst,
Equal in their creation they were formed,   690
Save what sin hath impaired, which yet hath wrought
Insensibly, for I suspend their doom;
Whence in perpetual fight they needs must last
Endless, and no solution will be found:
War wearied hath performed what war can do,   695
And to disordered rage let loose the reins,
With mountains as with weapons armed, which makes
Wild work in heav'n, and dangerous to the main.
Two days are therefore past, the third is thine;
For thee I have ordained it, and thus far   700

698. *the main.* The cosmos.

Have suffered, that the glory may be thine
Of ending this great war, since none but thou
Can end it. Into thee such virtue and grace
Immense I have transfused, that all may know
In heaven and hell thy power above compare,   705
And this perverse commotion governed thus,
To manifest thee worthiest to be heir
Of all things, to be heir and to be king
By sacred unction, thy deserved right.

Critics have noted flaws in God's reasoning. Since the Son receives all his power from the Father, he is not 'above compare' but inferior to the Father. Further, the fact that the Son can end the war, using his Father's invincible power, has no bearing on whether he is 'worthiest' or whether his kingship is 'deserved'.

The Son mounts the 'chariot of paternal deity', a mystical armoured vehicle with a biblical source (Ezekiel 1 and 10). He drives the Satanic army before him and, terrified, they throw themselves through a gap that opens in the wall of heaven into the 'bottomless pit' of hell. The heavenly host applaud the Son as he returns from his triumph.

Concluding his account of the war, Raphael delivers his warning to Adam as God instructed.

Thus measuring things in heaven by things on earth,
At thy request, and that thou mayst beware

701. *suffered.* Allowed the war to go on.

By what is past, to thee I have revealed   895
What might have else to human race been hid;
The discord which befell, and war in heaven
Among the angelic powers, and the deep fall
Of those too high aspiring, who rebelled
With Satan, he who envies now thy state,   900
Who now is plotting how he may seduce
Thee also from obedience, that with him
Bereaved of happiness thou mayst partake
His punishment, eternal misery;
Which would be all his solace and revenge,   905
As a despite done against the most high,
Thee once to gain companion of his woe.
But list'n not to his temptations, warn
Thy weaker; let it profit thee to have heard
By terrible example the reward   910
Of disobedience; firm they might have stood,
Yet fell; remember, and fear to transgress.

896. The war in heaven is not described in the Bible, and Milton may here be
claiming scriptural authority for the account the heavenly Muse has dictated to him.
909. *Thy weaker*. Eve.

BOOK 7

Milton starts Book 7 by addressing his Muse, Urania. He asks for her continued help, and laments his blindness, solitude and feelings of persecution.

Descend from heaven, Urania, by that name
If rightly thou art called, whose voice divine
Following, above the Olympian hill I soar,
Above the flight of Pegasean wing.
The meaning, not the name, I call: for thou   5
Nor of the Muses nine, nor on the top
Of old Olympus dwellst, but heav'nly born,
Before the hills appeared, or fountain flowed,
Thou with eternal Wisdom didst converse,
Wisdom thy sister, and with her didst play   10
In presence of the almighty Father, pleased
With thy celestial song. Up led by thee
Into the heav'n of heav'ns I have presumed,

1. Urania. See 'Milton's Muse', p. 11–15 *3. Olympian hill.* Mount Olympus, home of the classical Muses. *4. Pegasean.* Pegasus was a winged horse that flew to heaven in classical myth. *5. meaning.* Urania means 'heavenly'. *9. Wisdom.* In Proverbs 8:30 Wisdom is God's daughter, 'his delight, playing always before him', and is with him when he creates the world.

An earthly guest, and drawn empyreal air,
Thy tempering; with like safety guided down   15
Return me to my native element:
Lest from this flying steed unreined (as once
Bellerophon, though from a lower clime),
Dismounted, on the Aleian field I fall
Erroneous, there to wander and forlorn.   20
Half yet remains unsung, but narrower bound
Within the visible diurnal sphere;
Standing on earth, not rapt above the pole,
More safe I sing with mortal voice, unchanged
To hoarse or mute, though fallen on evil days,   25
On evil days though fallen, and evil tongues;
In darkness, and with dangers compassed round,
And solitude; yet not alone, while thou
Visitst my slumbers nightly, or when morn
Purples the east: still govern thou my song,   30
Urania, and fit audience find, though few.
But drive far off the barbarous dissonance
Of Bacchus and his revellers, the race
Of that wild rout that tore the Thracian bard

14–15. The fiery (*empyreal*) air of the empyrean (heaven) would need *tempering* to be
breathable by a human. *18. Bellerophon.* Tried to fly to heaven on Pegasus, and fell
on the plain of Aleion, blinded and crippled. *23. pole.* Pole star. *26. evil days.* After
the Restoration Milton was imprisoned and publicly derided. *34. Thracian bard.*
Orpheus, son of the *Muse* Calliope, whose music charmed *woods and rocks,* was torn to
pieces by female Bacchantes on the *Rhodope* Mountains.

In Rhodope, where woods and rocks had ears   35
To rapture, till the savage clamour drowned
Both harp and voice; nor could the Muse defend
Her son. So fail not thou, who thee implores
For thou art heav'nly, she an empty dream.

Milton's invocation of Urania ends, and the poem takes up the story
where Book 6 left off. Raphael is still in conversation with Adam in
the garden. Adam thanks him for his account of the war in heaven.
But he has another question. Can Raphael tell him how and why God
created the earth? Raphael agrees to try. After Satan and the evil
angels had been thrown out, he recounts, God the Father addressed
the Son, saying that enough angels still remained to populate heaven.
Satan, God continues, has taken one third of the angels:

But lest his heart exalt him in the harm   150
Already done, to have dispeopled heaven,
My damage fondly deemed, I can repair
That detriment, if such it be to lose
Self-lost, and in a moment will create
Another world, out of one man a race   155
Of men innumerable, there to dwell,
Not here, till by degrees of merit raised,
They open to themselves at length the way

152. *My damage fondly deemed.* Which Satan foolishly thinks has damaged me.
154. *Self-lost.* The fallen angels who have lost their original being.

THE ESSENTIAL PARADISE LOST

Up hither, under long obedience tried,
And earth be changed to heaven, and heaven to earth,   160
One kingdom, joy and union without end.
Meanwhile inhabit lax, ye powers of heaven,
And thou my Word, begotten Son, by thee
This I perform, speak thou, and be it done:
My overshadowing spirit and might with thee   165
I send along, ride forth, and bid the deep
Within appointed bounds be heaven and earth,
Boundless the deep, because I am who fill
Infinitude, nor vacuous the space.
Though I uncircumscribed myself retire,   170
And put not forth my goodness, which is free
To act or not, necessity and chance
Approach not me, and what I will is fate.
    So spake the almighty, and to what he spake
His Word, the filial Godhead, gave effect.   175
Immediate are the acts of God, more swift
Than time or motion, but to human ears
Cannot without process of speech be told,
So told as earthly notion can receive.

*God's explanation here of how he created heaven and earth is unortho-
dox, but tallies with Milton's own opinion. The orthodox view was that
God created heaven and earth out of nothing. Milton (in his treatise*

162. *inhabit lax.* Spread out.

Christian Doctrine) *argued that nothing could be made out of nothing,
and since God alone is infinite he must have made heaven, earth and hell
out of himself. By withdrawing his 'goodness' from part of himself he left
formless chaos, which became the raw material of creation.*

*When God had finished speaking, Raphael recounts, the heavenly
host glorified his creative plan, and the Son, with his angelic entourage,
left heaven's gate. Outside he confronted chaos ('dark, wasteful, wild').
But it grew quiet at his command, and with 'golden compasses' (from
Proverbs 8:27) he drew the circumference of the universe. Raphael's
account of creation follows the Genesis sequence. On the first day God
created light, and divided light from darkness; on the second, he created
the firmament and divided it from the waters; on the third he created the oceans and land masses and vegetation; on the fourth, the sun,
moon and stars; on the fifth, sea-life and birds.*

The sixth, and of creation last arose
With evening harps and matin, when God said,   450
Let the earth bring forth soul living in her kind,
Cattle and creeping things, and beast of the earth,
Each in their kind. The earth obeyed, and straight
Opening her fertile womb teemed at a birth
Innumerous living creatures, perfect forms,   455
Limbed and full grown: out of the ground up rose,
As from his lair the wild beast where he wons
In forest wild, in thicket, brake, or den;

450. *matin.* Morning.   457. *wons.* Lives.

Among the trees in pairs they rose, they walked:
The cattle in the fields and meadows green: 460
Those rare and solitary, these in flocks
Pasturing at once, and in broad herds upsprung.
The grassy clods now calved, now half appeared
The tawny lion, pawing to get free
His hinder parts, then springs as broke from bonds,   465
And rampant shakes his brinded mane; the ounce,
The leopard, and the tiger, as the mole
Rising, the crumbled earth above them threw
In hillocks: the swift stag from under ground
Bore up his branching head: scarce from his mould   470
Behemoth biggest born of earth upheaved
His vastness: fleeced the flocks and bleating rose,
As plants: ambiguous between sea and land
The river horse and scaly crocodile.
At once came forth whatever creeps the ground,   475
Insect or worm; those waved their limber fans
For wings, and smallest lineaments exact
In all the liveries decked of summer's pride
With spots of gold and purple, azure and green:
These as a line their long dimension drew,   480
Streaking the ground with sinuous trace; not all

461. *Those.* Wild animals. *rare.* Far apart. *these.* Domestic animals. *466. brinded.*
Dappled and tawny. *ounce.* Lynx. *471. Behemoth.* Mentioned in Job 40:15, perhaps
the elephant. *474. river horse.* Hippopotamus. *476. worm.* General term for creeping
things. *limber.* Flexible.

Minims of nature; some of serpent kind,
Wondrous in length and corpulence involved
Their snaky folds, and added wings. First crept
The parsimonious emmet, provident   485
Of future, in small room large heart enclosed,
Pattern of just equality perhaps
Hereafter, joined in her popular tribes
Of commonalty: swarming next appeared
The female bee that feeds her husband drone   490
Deliciously, and builds her waxen cells
With honey stored: the rest are numberless,
And thou their natures knowst, and gav'st them names,
Needless to thee repeated; nor unknown
The serpent subtlest beast of all the field,   495
Of huge extent sometimes, with brazen eyes
And hairy mane terrific, though to thee
Not noxious, but obedient at thy call.

*After the world had been created, Raphael recounts, God the Father said
to the Son, 'Let us now make man in our image'. So Adam and Eve
were created and the creator gave them dominion over all living things:*

    . . . as thou knowst
He brought thee into this delicious grove,

482. Minims. Miniatures. *486. emmet.* Ant, proverbial for thrift and public spirit.
493. thou. Adam. *gav'st them names.* As in Genesis 2:19. *498. noxious.* Harmful.

This garden, planted with the trees of God,
Delectable both to behold and taste;
And freely all their pleasant fruit for food   540
Gave thee, all sorts are here that all the earth yields,
Variety without end; but of the tree,
Which tasted works knowledge of good and evil,
Thou mayst not; in the day thou eatst, thou di'st;
Death is the penalty imposed; beware.   545

*In conclusion Raphael tells how the heavenly host sang God's praises
for his creation of the earth and the stars.*

    *The idea that there might be other populated worlds, besides the
earth, was common among seventeenth-century thinkers. It was a
theory that appealed to Milton, and the angels, as they sing, speculate
that 'every star' is 'perhaps a world/Of destined habitation'.*

BOOK 8

Adam thanks Raphael for his account of the creation. Unwilling to lose his heavenly guest's company, he asks for an explanation of the earth's relation to the sun and the stars. Raphael, however, does not encourage this line of enquiry. Knowing whether the earth moves, or the stars, is not important, he says. God, foreseeing the speculations of astronomers, has deliberately made the 'fabric of the heavens' a difficult subject, 'perhaps to move/His laughter at their quaint opinions wide'. The sun, Raphael goes on to suggest, may be the centre of the universe, and the earth one of the planets circling round it. However, he puts forward this outline of what was to become the Copernican theory as just one of many possibilities, none of which, he says, Adam needs to know about. What matters is for him to fear and obey God. Adam agrees and, changing the subject, asks if Raphael would like to hear what he remembers about being created. Raphael says he would, as he was not present to witness the creation:

For I that day was absent, as befell,
Bound on a voyage uncouth and obscure,   230
Far on excursion toward the gates of hell;
Squared in full legion (such command we had)

230. *uncouth.* Unknown.

To see that none thence issued forth a spy,
Or enemy, while God was in his work;
Lest he incensed at such eruption bold,   235
Destruction with creation might have mixed.
Not that they durst without his leave attempt,
But us he sends upon his high behests
_For state, as sovereign king, and to inure
Our prompt obedience.   240

So Adam tells Raphael about his first moments of conscious life:

As new waked from soundest sleep,
Soft on the flowery herb I found me laid
In balmy sweat, which with his beams the sun   255
Soon dried, and on the reeking moisture fed.
Straight toward heaven my wondering eyes I turned,
And gazed a while the ample sky, till raised
By quick instinctive motion up I sprung,
As thitherward endeavouring, and upright   260
Stood on my feet: about me round I saw
Hill, dale, and shady woods, and sunny plains,
And liquid lapse of murmuring streams, by these
Creatures that lived, and moved, and walked, or flew,
Birds on the branches warbling; all things smiled   265
With fragrance and with joy my heart o'erflowed.

256. reeking. Steaming. *260. thitherward.* Towards the sky.

Myself I then perused, and limb by limb
Surveyed, and sometimes went, and sometimes ran
With supple joints, as lively vigour led:
But who I was, or where, or from what cause,　　　　　　270
Knew not; to speak I tried, and forthwith spake,
My tongue obeyed and readily could name
Whate'er I saw. Thou sun, said I, fair light,
And thou enlightened earth, so fresh and gay,
Ye hills and dales, ye rivers, woods, and plains,　　　　275
And ye that live and move, fair creatures, tell,
Tell, if ye saw, how I came thus, how here?
Not of myself; by some great maker then,
In goodness and in power pre-eminent;
Tell me, how may I know him, how adore,　　　　　　280
From whom I have that thus I move and live,
And feel that I am happier than I know.
While thus I called, and strayed I knew not whither,
From where I first drew air, and first beheld
This happy light, when, answer none returned,　　　　285
On a green shady bank profuse of flowers,
Pensive I sat me down; there gentle sleep
First found me, and with soft oppression seized
My drowsed sense, untroubled, though I thought
I then was passing to my former state　　　　　　　290
Insensible, and forthwith to dissolve:

268. *went.* Walked.　*285. answer none returned.* No answer [having been] returned.

When suddenly stood at my head a dream,
Whose inward apparition gently moved
My fancy to believe I yet had being,
And lived: one came, methought, of shape divine,   295
And said, Thy mansion wants thee, Adam, rise,
First man, of men innumerable ordained
First father, called by thee I come thy guide
To the garden of bliss, thy seat prepared.
So saying, by the hand he took me raised,   300
And over fields and waters, as in air
Smooth sliding without step, last led me up
A woody mountain whose high top was plain,
A circuit wide, enclosed, with goodliest trees
Planted, with walks, and bowers, that what I saw   305
Of earth before scarce pleasant seemed. Each tree,
Loaden with fairest fruit, that hung to the eye
Tempting, stirred in me sudden appetite
To pluck and eat; whereat I waked, and found
Before mine eyes all real, as the dream   310
Had lively shadowed: here had new begun
My wandering, had not he who was my guide
Up hither, from among the trees appeared,
Presence divine. Rejoicing, but with awe
In adoration at his feet I fell   315
Submiss: he reared me, and Whom thou soughtst I am,

296. *Thy mansion wants thee.* Your home lacks your presence.

Said mildly, author of all this thou seest
Above, or round about thee or beneath.
This Paradise I give thee, count it thine
To till and keep, and of the fruit to eat: 320
Of every tree that in the garden grows
Eat freely with glad heart; fear here no dearth.
But of the tree whose operation brings
Knowledge of good and ill, which I have set,
The pledge of thy obedience and thy faith,   325
Amid the garden by the tree of life,
Remember what I warn thee, shun to taste,
And shun the bitter consequence: for know,
The day thou eatst thereof, my sole command
Transgressed, inevitably thou shalt die;   330
From that day mortal, and this happy state
Shalt lose, expelled from hence into a world
Of woe and sorrow. Sternly he pronounced
The rigid interdiction, which resounds
Yet dreadful in mine ear, though in my choice   335
Not to incur; but soon his clear aspect
Returned, and gracious purpose thus renewed.
Not only these fair bounds, but all the earth
To thee and to thy race I give; as lords
Possess it, and all things that therein live,   340
Or live in sea, or air; beast, fish, and fowl.

335–6. Though . . . incur. Although I did not mean to disobey.

In sign whereof, each bird and beast behold
After their kinds; I bring them to receive
From thee their names, and pay thee fealty
With low subjection; understand the same   345
Of fish within their watery residence,
Not hither summoned, since they cannot change
Their element to draw the thinner air.
As thus he spake, each bird and beast behold
Approaching two and two, these cowering low   350
With blandishment, each bird stooped on his wing.
I named them, as they passed, and understood
Their nature, with such knowledge God endued
My sudden apprehension: but in these
I found not what methought I wanted still;   355
And to the heavenly vision thus presumed.

   O by what name, for thou above all these,
Above mankind, or aught than mankind higher,
Surpassest far my naming, how may I
Adore thee, author of this universe,   360
And all this good to man, for whose well-being
So amply, and with hands so liberal,
Thou hast provided all things: but with me
I see not who partakes. In solitude
What happiness, who can enjoy alone,   365
Or all enjoying, what contentment find?

354. sudden apprehension. Instant understanding.

Thus I presumptuous; and the vision bright,
As with a smile more brightened, thus replied.
  What callst thou solitude, is not the earth
With various living creatures, and the air   370
Replenished, and all these at thy command
To come and play before thee, knowst thou not
Their language and their ways, they also know,
And reason not contemptibly: with these
Find pastime, and bear rule; thy realm is large.   375
So spake the universal Lord, and seemed
So ordering. I with leave of speech implored,
And humble deprecation thus replied.
  Let not my words offend thee, heavenly power,
My maker, be propitious while I speak.   380
Hast thou not made me here thy substitute,
And these inferior far beneath me set?
Among unequals what society
Can sort, what harmony or true delight?
Which must be mutual, in proportion due   385
Given and received; but in disparity
The one intense, the other still remiss,
Cannot well suit with either, but soon prove
Tedious alike: of fellowship I speak

372–3. *Knowst . . . language.* There was an ancient Jewish belief that until the Fall
Adam understood the language of birds and animals. *378. deprecation.* Apology.
387. Adam contrasts keen (*intense*) human intelligence with that of animals, which is
relatively deficient (*remiss*).

Such as I seek, fit to participate   390
All rational delight, wherein the brute
Cannot be human consort; they rejoice
Each with their kind, lion with lioness;
So fitly them in pairs thou hast combined;
Much less can bird with beast, or fish with fowl   395
So well converse, nor with the ox the ape;
Worse then can man with beast, and least of all.
   Whereto the almighty answered, not displeased.
A nice and subtle happiness I see,
Thou to thyself proposest, in the choice   400
Of thy associates, Adam, and wilt taste
No pleasure, though in pleasure, solitary.
What thinkst thou then of me, and this my state,
Seem I to thee sufficiently possessed
Of happiness, or not? Who am alone   405
From all eternity; for none I know
Second to me or like, equal much less.
How have I then with whom to hold converse
Save with the creatures which I made, and those
To me inferior, infinite descents   410
Beneath what other creatures are to thee?
   He ceased, I lowly answered. To attain
The height and depth of thy eternal ways

---

399. nice. Fastidious. *402. though in pleasure.* Though in Eden (meaning 'pleasure' in Hebrew).

All human thoughts come short, supreme of things!
Thou in thyself art perfect, and in thee   415
Is no deficience found; not so is man,
But in degree, the cause of his desire
By conversation with his like to help,
Or solace his defects. No need that thou
Shouldst propagate, already infinite;   420
And through all numbers absolute, though one:
But man by number is to manifest
His single imperfection, and beget
Like of his like, his image multiplied,
In unity defective, which requires   425
Collateral love, and dearest amity.
Thou in thy secrecy, although alone,
Best with thyself accompanied, seekst not
Social communication, yet, so pleased,
Canst raise thy creature to what height thou wilt   430
Of union or communion, deified:
I by conversing cannot these erect
From prone, nor in their ways complacence find.

God replies that he has only been pretending, in order to 'try' Adam,
and that he always intended to create a mate for him. He puts Adam
to sleep, but leaves his 'internal sight' open. So he is aware that God

417. But in degree. Or only partially. *423. His single imperfection.* The fact that he is
imperfect when alone. *429. So pleased.* If you choose. *431. deified.* Raised to divine
status.

[141]

takes a rib from his side and forms it into a creature so beautiful that everything else in the world seems inferior to her. When he awakes, Eve is there before him, and he leads her to their 'nuptial bower', giving thanks to God.

Completing his creation story, Adam admits to Raphael that Eve's beauty affects him in a way that causes him some anxiety:

Thus I have told thee all my state, and brought
My story to the sum of earthly bliss,
Which I enjoy, and must confess to find
In all things else delight indeed, but such
As used or not, works in the mind no change,   525
Nor vehement desire, these delicacies
I mean of taste, sight, smell, herbs, fruits, and flowers,
Walks, and the melody of birds; but here
Far otherwise, transported I behold,
Transported touch; here passion first I felt,   530
Commotion strange, in all enjoyments else
Superior and unmoved, here only weak
Against the charm of beauty's powerful glance.
Or nature failed in me, and left some part
Not proof enough such object to sustain,   535
Or from my side subducting, took perhaps
More than enough; at least on her bestowed

528. here. In Eve's presence. *534–6. Or . . . Or.* Either . . . Or. *536. subducting.* Subtracting.

Too much of ornament, in outward show
Elaborate, of inward less exact.
For well I understand in the prime end   540
Of nature her the inferior, in the mind
And inward faculties, which most excel,
In outward also her resembling less
His image who made both, and less expressing
The character of that dominion given   545
O'er other creatures; yet when I approach
Her loveliness, so absolute she seems
And in herself complete, so well to know
Her own, that what she wills to do or say,
Seems wisest, virtuousest, discreetest, best: 550
All higher knowledge in her presence falls
Degraded, wisdom in discourse with her
Loses discountenanced, and like folly shows;
Authority and reason on her wait,
As one intended first, not after made   555
Occasionally; and to consummate all,
Greatness of mind and nobleness their seat
Build in her loveliest, and create an awe
About her, as a guard angelic placed.
To whom the angel with contracted brow.   560
    Accuse not nature, she hath done her part;
Do thou but thine, and be not diffident

556. *Occasionally.* Incidentally.   562. *diffident.* Distrustful.

Of wisdom, she deserts thee not, if thou
Dismiss not her, when most thou needst her nigh,
By attributing overmuch to things   565
Less excellent, as thou thyself perceiv'st.
For what admir'st thou, what transports thee so,
An outside? Fair no doubt, and worthy well
Thy cherishing, thy honouring, and thy love,
Not thy subjection: weigh with her thyself;   570
Then value: oft-times nothing profits more
Than self-esteem, grounded on just and right
Well managed; of that skill the more thou knowst,
The more she will acknowledge thee her head,
And to realities yield all her shows: 575
Made so adorn for thy delight the more,
So awful, that with honour thou mayst love
Thy mate, who sees when thou art seen least wise.
But if the sense of touch whereby mankind
Is propagated seem such dear delight   580
Beyond all other, think the same vouchsafed
To cattle and each beast; which would not be
To them made common and divulged, if aught
Therein enjoyed were worthy to subdue
The soul of man, or passion in him move.   585
What higher in her society thou findst
Attractive, human, rational, love still;

576. *adorn.* Adorned (Milton's coinage).   577. *awful.* Awesome.

[144]

In loving thou dost well, in passion not,
Wherein true love consists not; love refines
The thoughts, and heart enlarges; hath his seat   590
In reason, and is judicious, is the scale
By which to heavenly love thou mayst ascend,
Not sunk in carnal pleasure; for which cause
Among the beasts no mate for thee was found.
   To whom thus half abashed Adam replied.   595
Neither her outside formed so fair, nor aught
In procreation common to all kinds
(Though higher of the genial bed by far,
And with mysterious reverence I deem)
So much delights me, as those graceful acts,   600
Those thousand decencies that daily flow
From all her words and actions, mixed with love
And sweet compliance, which declare unfeigned
Union of mind, or in us both one soul;
Harmony to behold in wedded pair   605
More grateful than harmonious sound to the ear.
Yet these subject not; I to thee disclose
What inward thence I feel, not therefore foiled,
Who meet with various objects, from the sense
Variously representing; yet still free,   610
Approve the best, and follow what I approve.

---

598. genial. Relating to marriage and childbirth.   *601. decencies.* Becoming qualities.
607. subject not. Do not dominate me.   *608. foiled.* Overcome, degraded.

To love thou blam'st me not; for love thou sayst,
Leads up to heaven, is both the way and guide;
Bear with me then, if lawful what I ask;
Love not the heavenly spirits, and how their love   615
Express they, by looks only, or do they mix
Irradiance, virtual or immediate touch?
   To whom the angel with a smile that glowed
Celestial rosy red, love's proper hue,
Answered. Let it suffice thee that thou knowst   620
Us happy, and without love no happiness.
Whatever pure thou in the body enjoyst,
(And pure thou wert created) we enjoy
In eminence; and obstacle find none
Of membrane, joint, or limb, exclusive bars: 625
Easier than air with air, if spirits embrace,
Total they mix, union of pure with pure
Desiring, nor restrained conveyance need
As flesh to mix with flesh, or soul with soul.
But I can now no more; the parting sun   630
Beyond the earth's green cape and verdant Isles
Hesperean sets, my signal to depart.
Be strong, live happy, and love, but first of all
Him whom to love is to obey, and keep
His great command; take heed lest passion sway   635

616–17. *mix Irradiance.* Mingle their radiant beings. 619. *proper.* Appropriate. 632.
Hesperean. Western.

Thy judgement to do aught, which else free will
Would not admit; thine and of all thy sons
The weal or woe in thee is placed; beware.
I in thy persevering shall rejoice,
And all the blest: stand fast; to stand or fall   640
Free in thine own arbitrament it lies.
Perfect within, no outward aid require;
And all temptation to transgress repel.

*Raphael flies back to heaven, and Book 9 takes up the story with Adam
and Eve, duly warned, in the garden.*

640. the blest. The heavenly host. *641. arbitrament.* Choice.

BOOK 9

Milton introduces the final phase of his poem, which will narrate the fall of man and God's judgement. He defends his choice of subject as 'more heroic' than Homer's Iliad, *Virgil's* Aeneid *and more recent chivalric epics. Giving a brief run-down of the typical contents of such poems, he declares them unsuited to his skills and temperament. He once more registers his indebtedness to his Muse who 'dictates'* Paradise Lost *to him each night, while he is 'slumbering'.*

No more of talk where God or angel guest
With man, as with his friend, familiar used
To sit indulgent, and with him partake
Rural repast, permitting him the while
Venial discourse unblamed. I now must change   5
Those notes to tragic; foul distrust, and breach
Disloyal on the part of man, revolt,
And disobedience: on the part of heaven
Now alienated, distance and distaste,
Anger and just rebuke, and judgement given,   10
That brought into this world a world of woe,
Sin and her shadow Death, and misery

---

5. *Venial*. Allowed. *9. distaste*. Revulsion.

Death's harbinger: sad task, yet argument
Not less but more heroic than the wrath
Of stern Achilles on his foe pursued   15
Thrice fugitive about Troy wall; or rage
Of Turnus for Lavinia disespoused,
Or Neptune's ire or Juno's, that so long
Perplexed the Greek and Cytherea's son:
If answerable style I can obtain   20
Of my celestial patroness, who deigns
Her nightly visitation unimplored,
And dictates to me slumbering, or inspires
Easy my unpremeditated verse:
Since first this subject for heroic song   25
Pleased me long choosing, and beginning late;
Not sedulous by nature to indite
Wars, hitherto the only argument
Heroic deemed, chief mastery to dissect
With long and tedious havoc fabled knights   30
In battles feigned; the better fortitude
Of patience and heroic martyrdom
Unsung; or to describe races and games,
Or tilting furniture, emblazoned shields,

---

13. harbinger. Herald. *14–19.* Referring to Homer's *Iliad* and Virgil's *Aeneid.* *14. his foe.* Hector. *19. the Greek.* Odysseus. *Cytherea's son.* Aeneas. *26. long choosing.* Milton had originally planned to write an epic about King Arthur. *27. sedulous.* Keen. *indite.* Write about. *33. heroic martyrdom.* The Son's voluntary death to save mankind. *34. tilting furniture.* Jousting equipment.

Impreses quaint, caparisons and steeds;   35
Bases and tinsel trappings, gorgeous knights
At joust and tournament; then marshalled feast
Served up in hall with sewers, and seneschals;
The skill of artifice or office mean,
Not that which justly gives heroic name   40
To person or to poem. Me of these
Nor skilled nor studious, higher argument
Remains, sufficient of itself to raise
That name, unless an age too late, or cold
Climate, or years damp my intended wing   45
Depressed, and much they may, if all be mine,
Not hers who brings it nightly to my ear.

*Finishing his introduction, Milton takes up the story with Satan
slinking back into the garden under cover of night. Looking for a disguise, he takes on the form of a snake. But first he gives voice to the
hatred the earth's beauty inspires in him.*

O earth, how like to heaven, if not preferred
More justly, seat worthier of gods, as built   100
With second thoughts, reforming what was old!
For what god after better worse would build?

35. *Impreses.* Heraldic emblems. *36. Bases.* Embroidered cloth worn over armour. *38.
sewers . . . seneschals.* Waiters and stewards. *39. The . . . mean.* An unworthy use of art
or effort. *44. That name.* Heroic.

Terrestrial heaven, danced round by other heavens
That shine, yet bear their bright officious lamps,
Light above light, for thee alone, as seems,   105
In thee concentring all their precious beams
Of sacred influence; as God in heaven
Is centre, yet extends to all, so thou,
Centring, receiv'st from all those orbs: in thee,
Not in themselves, all their known virtue appears   110
Productive in herb, plant, and nobler birth
Of creatures animate with gradual life
Of growth, sense, reason, all summed up in man.
With what delight could I have walked thee round,
If I could joy in aught, sweet interchange   115
Of hill and valley, rivers, woods, and plains,
Now land, now sea, and shores with forest crowned,
Rocks, dens, and caves; but I in none of these
Find place or refuge; and the more I see
Pleasures about me, so much more I feel   120
Torment within me, as from the hateful siege
Of contraries; all good to me becomes
Bane, and in heaven much worse would be my state.
But neither here seek I, no nor in heaven
To dwell, unless by mastering heaven's supreme;   125
Nor hope to be myself less miserable
By what I seek, but others to make such

---

112. gradual. Arranged in degrees. *123. Bane.* Poison. *125. heaven's supreme.* God.

As I, though thereby worse to me redound:
For only in destroying I find ease
To my relentless thoughts; and, him destroyed,   130
Or won to what may work his utter loss,
For whom all this was made, all this will soon
Follow, as to him linked in weal or woe;
In woe then, that destruction wide may range:
To me shall be the glory sole among   135
The infernal powers, in one day to have marred
What he, almighty styled, six nights and days
Continued making, and who knows how long
Before had been contriving, though perhaps
Not longer than since I in one night freed   140
From servitude inglorious well nigh half
The angelic name, and thinner left the throng
Of his adorers: he to be avenged,
And to repair his numbers thus impaired,
Whether such virtue spent of old now failed   145
More angels to create, if they at least
Are his created, or to spite us more,
Determined to advance into our room
A creature formed of earth, and him endow,
Exalted from so base original,   150
With heavenly spoils, our spoils: what he decreed,

---

130. *him.* Man. *141. well nigh half.* Actually a third. *146–7. if . . . created.*
Contradicting what he admitted in Book 4:43. *151. spoils.* Endowments.

THE ESSENTIAL PARADISE LOST

He effected; man he made, and for him built
Magnificent this world, and earth his seat,
Him lord pronounced; and, oh indignity!
Subjected to his service angel wings,   155
And flaming ministers to watch and tend
Their earthy charge: of these the vigilance
I dread, and to elude, thus wrapped in mist
Of midnight vapour glide obscure, and pry
In every bush and brake, where hap may find   160
The serpent sleeping, in whose mazy folds
To hide me, and the dark intent I bring.
Oh foul descent! That I who erst contended
With gods to sit the highest, am now constrained
Into a beast, and mixed with bestial slime,   165
This essence to incarnate and imbrute,
That to the height of deity aspired;
But what will not ambition and revenge
Descend to? Who aspires must down as low
As high he soared, obnoxious first or last,   170
To basest things. Revenge, at first though sweet,
Bitter ere long back on itself recoils;
Let it; I reck not, so it light well aimed,
Since higher I fall short, on him who next
Provokes my envy, this new favourite   175

163. erst. Formerly. *170. obnoxious.* Exposed. *173. reck.* Care. *174. Since . . . short.* Since
I cannot attack God directly.

Of heaven, this man of clay, son of despite,
Whom us the more to spite his maker raised
From dust: spite then with spite is best repaid.

*Searching the garden, Satan finds the serpent asleep and slips into its
body through the mouth.*

*With the coming of morning, Adam and Eve prepare for their day's
gardening. The garden's rampant growth is more than they can control, and Eve suggests that it would be more efficient if they worked
separately in different parts of the garden. Adam is against this, as he
fears she will be less able to withstand temptation if he is not by her
side. Realising that he fears this, Eve expresses her hurt, and Adam,
because he is so in love, denies that he mistrusts her, and fatally allows
her to go off alone.*

Meanwhile Satan searches the garden for his human prey.

He sought them both, but wished his hap might find
Eve separate, he wished, but not with hope
Of what so seldom chanced, when to his wish,
Beyond his hope, Eve separate he spies,
Veiled in a cloud of fragrance, where she stood,   425
Half spied, so thick the roses blushing round
About her glowed, oft stooping to support
Each flower of slender stalk, whose head though gay
Carnation, purple, azure, or specked with gold,
Hung drooping unsustained, them she upstays   430
Gently with myrtle band, mindless the while,

Herself, though fairest unsupported flower,
From her best prop so far, and storm so nigh.
Nearer he drew, and many a walk traversed
Of stateliest covert, cedar, pine, or palm,   435
Then voluble and bold, now hid, now seen
Among thick-woven arborets and flowers
Embordered on each bank, the hand of Eve:
Spot more delicious than those gardens feigned
Or of revived Adonis, or renowned   440
Alcinous, host of old Laertes' son,
Or that, not mystic, where the sapient king
Held dalliance with his fair Egyptian spouse.
Much he the place admired, the person more.
As one who long in populous city pent,   445
Where houses thick and sewers annoy the air,
Forth issuing on a summer's morn, to breathe
Among the pleasant villages and farms
Adjoined, from each thing met conceives delight,
The smell of grain, or tedded grass, or kine,   450
Or dairy, each rural sight, each rural sound;
If chance with nymph-like step fair virgin pass,
What pleasing seemed, for her now pleases more,

---

436. voluble. In coils. *437. arborets.* Bushes. *438. hand.* Handiwork. *440.* As part of
the Adonis cult, Athenian women sowed annual gardens. *441. Laertes' son.* Odysseus,
who admires *Alcinous's* garden in the *Odyssey. 442. mystic.* Fictional. *sapient king.*
Solomon. *443. Egyptian spouse.* Pharaoh's daughter, one of Solomon's many wives.
450. tedded. Spread to dry. *kine.* Cattle.

She most, and in her look sums all delight.
Such pleasure took the serpent to behold   455
This flowery plat, the sweet recess of Eve
Thus early, thus alone: her heavenly form
Angelic, but more soft and feminine,
Her graceful innocence, her every air
Of gesture or least action overawed   460
His malice, and with rapine sweet bereaved
His fierceness of the fierce intent it brought:
That space the evil one abstracted stood
From his own evil, and for the time remained
Stupidly good; of enmity disarmed,   465
Of guile, of hate, of envy, of revenge;
But the hot hell that always in him burns,
Though in mid-heaven, soon ended his delight,
And tortures him now more, the more he sees
Of pleasure not for him ordained: then soon   470
Fierce hate he recollects, and all his thoughts
Of mischief, gratulating, thus excites.
     Thoughts, whither have ye led me! with what sweet
Compulsion thus transported to forget
What hither brought us, hate, not love, nor hope   475
Of Paradise for hell, hope here to taste
Of pleasure, but all pleasure to destroy,
Save what is in destroying, other joy

456. *plat*. Plot.   465. *Stupidly*. As stupefied.   472. *gratulating*. Rejoicing in.

To me is lost. Then let me not let pass
Occasion which now smiles, behold alone   480
The woman, opportune to all attempts,
Her husband, for I view far round, not nigh,
Whose higher intellectual more I shun,
And strength, of courage haughty, and of limb
Heroic built, though of terrestrial mould,   485
Foe not informidable, exempt from wound,
I not: so much hath hell debased, and pain
Enfeebled me, to what I was in heaven.
She fair, divinely fair, fit love for gods,
Not terrible, though terror be in love   490
And beauty, not approached by stronger hate,
Hate stronger, under show of love well feigned,
The way which to her ruin now I tend.
    So spake the enemy of mankind, enclosed
In serpent, inmate bad, and toward Eve   495
Addressed his way, not with indented wave,
Prone on the ground, as since; but on his rear,
Circular base of rising folds, that towered
Fold above fold a surging maze, his head
Crested aloft, and carbuncle his eyes;   500
With burnished neck of verdant gold, erect
Amidst his circling spires, that on the grass

483. *intellectual.* Intellect. *488. to.* Compared to. *497. as since.* As snakes do now.

Floated redundant: pleasing was his shape,
And lovely; never since of serpent kind
Lovelier, not those that in Illyria changed   505
Hermione and Cadmus, or the god
In Epidaurus; nor to which transformed
Ammonian Jove, or Capitoline was seen;
He with Olympias, this with her who bore
Scipio the height of Rome. With tract oblique   510
At first, as one who sought access, but feared
To interrupt, sidelong he works his way.
As when a ship by skilful steersman wrought
Nigh river's mouth or foreland, where the wind
Veers oft, as oft so steers, and shifts her sail;   515
So varied he, and of his tortuous train
Curled many a wanton wreath in sight of Eve,
To lure her eye; she, busied, heard the sound
Of rustling leaves, but minded not, as used
To such disport before her through the field,   520
From every beast; more duteous at her call,
Than at Circean call the herd disguised.
He bolder now, uncalled before her stood,
But as in gaze admiring; oft he bowed

503. *redundant.* Overflowing. *505–10. Hermione,* goddess of harmony, and her
husband *Cadmus* changed into snakes. So did Aesculapius, *god* of healing, and Jupiter,
who had shrines at *Ammon* and on the *Capitoline,* and mated with *Olympias,* mother
of Alexander the Great and Pomponia, mother of *Scipio* Africanus. *522. Circean.* In
Homer's *Odyssey* Circe turns men to beasts.

His turret crest, and sleek enamelled neck,   525
Fawning; and licked the ground whereon she trod.
His gentle dumb expression turned at length
The eye of Eve to mark his play; he glad
Of her attention gained, with serpent-tongue
Organic, or impulse of vocal air,   530
His fraudulent temptation thus began.
    Wonder not, sovereign mistress, if perhaps
Thou canst, who art sole wonder, much less arm
Thy looks, the heaven of mildness, with disdain,
Displeased that I approach thee thus, and gaze   535
Insatiate, I thus single, nor have feared
Thy awful brow, more awful thus retired.
Fairest resemblance of thy maker fair,
Thee all things living gaze on, all things thine
By gift, and thy celestial beauty adore   540
With ravishment beheld, there best beheld
Where universally admired; but here
In this enclosure wild, these beasts among,
Beholders rude, and shallow to discern
Half what in thee is fair, one man except,   545
Who sees thee? (And what is one?) Who should be seen
A goddess among gods, adored and served
By angels numberless, thy daily train.
    So glozed the tempter, and his proem tuned:

536. *Insatiate.* Insatiable.   537. *awful.* Awe-inspiring.   549. *proem.* Prologue.

Into the heart of Eve his words made way,   550
Though at the voice much marvelling; at length
Not unamazed she thus in answer spake.
   What may this mean? Language of man pronounced
By tongue of brute, and human sense expressed?
The first at least of these I thought denied   555
To beasts; whom God on their creation-day
Created mute to all articulate sound;
The latter I demur, for in their looks
Much reason, and in their actions oft appears.
Thee, serpent, subtlest beast of all the field   560
I knew, but not with human voice endued;
Redouble then this miracle, and say,
How cam'st thou speakable of mute, and how
To me so friendly grown above the rest
Of brutal kind, that daily are in sight?   565
Say, for such wonder claims attention due.
   To whom the guileful tempter thus replied.
Empress of this fair world, resplendent Eve,
Easy to me it is to tell thee all
What thou commandst, and right thou shouldst be obeyed: 570
I was at first as other beasts that graze
The trodden herb, of abject thoughts and low,
As was my food; nor aught but food discerned
Or sex, and apprehended nothing high:

558. *demur.* Suspend judgement on.

[161]

Till on a day roving the field, I chanced   575
A goodly tree far distant to behold
Loaden with fruit of fairest colours mixed,
Ruddy and gold: I nearer drew to gaze;
When from the boughs a savoury odour blown,
Grateful to appetite, more pleased my sense   580
Than smell of sweetest fennel, or the teats
Of ewe or goat dropping with milk at even,
Unsucked of lamb or kid, that tend their play.
To satisfy the sharp desire I had
Of tasting those fair apples, I resolved   585
Not to defer; hunger and thirst at once,
Powerful persuaders, quickened at the scent
Of that alluring fruit, urged me so keen.
About the mossy trunk I wound me soon;
For high from ground the branches would require   590
Thy utmost reach or Adam's: round the tree
All other beasts that saw, with like desire
Longing and envying stood, but could not reach.
Amid the tree now got, where plenty hung
Tempting so nigh, to pluck and eat my fill   595
I spared not; for such pleasure till that hour
At feed or fountain never had I found.
Sated at length, ere long I might perceive
Strange alteration in me, to degree

581–2. Serpents were known to like *fennel* and sucking milk from farm animals.

Of reason in my inward powers; and speech   600
Wanted not long; though to this shape retained.
Thenceforth to speculations high or deep
I turned my thoughts, and with capacious mind
Considered all things visible in heaven,
Or earth, or middle; all things fair and good;   605
But all that fair and good in thy divine
Semblance, and in thy beauty's heavenly ray,
United I beheld; no fair to thine
Equivalent or second, which compelled
Me thus, though importune perhaps, to come   610
And gaze, and worship thee of right declared
Sovereign of creatures, universal dame.
    So talked the spirited sly snake; and Eve
Yet more amazed unwary thus replied.
    Serpent, thy overpraising leaves in doubt   615
The virtue of that fruit, in thee first proved:
But say, where grows the tree, from hence how far?
For many are the trees of God that grow
In Paradise, and various, yet unknown
To us; in such abundance lies our choice,   620
As leaves a greater store of fruit untouched,
Still hanging incorruptible, till men
Grow up to their provision, and more hands
Help to disburden nature of her birth.

---

601. *Wanted.* Was lacking. 608. *fair.* Beauty. 616. *virtue.* Power. *proved.* Tested.

To whom the wily adder, blithe and glad.   625
Empress, the way is ready, and not long,
Beyond a row of myrtles, on a flat,
Fast by a fountain, one small thicket past
Of blowing myrrh and balm; if thou accept
My conduct, I can bring thee thither soon.   630
   Lead then, said Eve. He leading swiftly rolled
In tangles, and made intricate seem straight,
To mischief swift. Hope elevates, and joy
Brightens his crest; as when a wandering fire
Compact of unctuous vapour, which the night   635
Condenses, and the cold environs round,
Kindled through agitation to a flame,
Which oft, they say, some evil spirit attends,
Hovering and blazing with delusive light,
Misleads the amazed night-wanderer from his way   640
To bogs and mires, and oft through pond or pool,
There swallowed up and lost, from succour far.
So glistered the dire snake, and into fraud
Led Eve, our credulous mother, to the tree
Of prohibition, root of all our woe;   645
Which when she saw, thus to her guide she spake.
   Serpent, we might have spared our coming hither,
Fruitless to me, though fruit be here to excess,
The credit of whose virtue rest with thee;

---

634. *wandering fire.* Natural phosphorescence, called *ignis fatuus.*   635. *unctuous.* Oily.

Wondrous indeed, if cause of such effects.   650
But of this tree we may not taste nor touch;
God so commanded, and left that command
Sole daughter of his voice; the rest, we live
Law to our selves, our reason is our law.
　　To whom the tempter guilefully replied.   655
Indeed! Hath God then said that of the fruit
Of all these garden trees ye shall not eat,
Yet lords declared of all in earth or air?
　　To whom thus Eve yet sinless. Of the fruit
Of each tree in the garden we may eat;   660
But of the fruit of this fair tree amidst
The garden, God hath said, Ye shall not eat
Thereof, nor shall ye touch it, lest ye die.
　　She scarce had said, though brief, when now more bold
The tempter, but with show of zeal and love   665
To man, and indignation at his wrong,
New part puts on; and as to passion moved,
Fluctuates disturbed, yet comely, and in act
Raised, as of some great matter to begin.
As when of old some orator renowned   670
In Athens or free Rome, where eloquence
Flourished, since mute, to some great cause addressed,
Stood in himself collected; while each part,

673–4. *Each part, Motion.* Each part [won] motion; referring to the orator's bodily gestures.

[165]

Motion, each act won audience ere the tongue,
Sometimes in height began, as no delay   675
Of preface brooking through his zeal of right.
So standing, moving, or to height upgrown
The tempter all impassioned thus began.

  O sacred, wise, and wisdom-giving plant,
Mother of science, now I feel thy power   680
Within me clear, not only to discern
Things in their causes, but to trace the ways
Of highest agents, deemed however wise.
Queen of this universe, do not believe
Those rigid threats of death; ye shall not die: 685
How should ye? By the fruit? It gives you life
To knowledge. By the threatener? Look on me,
Me who have touched and tasted, yet both live,
And life more perfect have attained than fate
Meant me, by venturing higher than my lot.   690
Shall that be shut to man, which to the beast
Is open? Or will God incense his ire
For such a petty trespass, and not praise
Rather your dauntless virtue, whom the pain
Of death denounced, whatever thing death be,   695
Deterred not from achieving what might lead
To happier life, knowledge of good and evil;
Of good, how just? Of evil, if what is evil

676. brooking. Tolerating. *694. virtue.* Courage.

Be real, why not known, since easier shunned?
God therefore cannot hurt ye, and be just;   700
Not just, not God; not feared then, nor obeyed:
Your fear itself of death removes the fear.
Why then was this forbid? Why but to awe,
Why but to keep ye low and ignorant,
His worshippers; he knows that in the day   705
Ye eat thereof, your eyes that seem so clear,
Yet are but dim, shall perfectly be then
Opened and cleared, and ye shall be as gods,
Knowing both good and evil as they know.
That ye should be as gods, since I as man,   710
Internal man, is but proportion meet,
I of brute human; ye of human gods.
So ye shall die perhaps, by putting off
Human, to put on gods, death to be wished,
Though threatened, which no worse than this can bring.   715
And what are gods that man may not become
As they, participating godlike food?
The gods are first, and that advantage use
On our belief, that all from them proceeds;
I question it; for this fair earth I see,   720
Warmed by the sun, producing every kind,
Them nothing: if they all things, who enclosed

---

719. *our belief.* The credulity of lesser creatures like snakes and humans. 722. *Them nothing.* While they produce nothing. *If they all things.* If they [produced] all things.

Knowledge of good and evil in this tree,
That whoso eats thereof, forthwith attains
Wisdom without their leave? And wherein lies   725
The offence, that man should thus attain to know?
What can your knowledge hurt him, or this tree
Impart against his will if all be his?
Or is it envy, and can envy dwell
In heavenly breasts? These, these and many more   730
Causes import your need of this fair fruit.
Goddess humane, reach then, and freely taste.

   He ended; and his words replete with guile,
Into her heart too easy entrance won:
Fixed on the fruit she gazed, which to behold   735
Might tempt alone, and in her ears the sound
Yet rung of his persuasive words, impregned
With reason, to her seeming, and with truth:
Meanwhile the hour of noon drew on, and waked
An eager appetite, raised by the smell   740
So savoury of that fruit, which with desire,
Inclinable now grown to touch or taste,
Solicited her longing eye; yet first
Pausing awhile, thus to herself she mused.

   Great are thy virtues, doubtless, best of fruits,   745
Though kept from man, and worthy to be admired;
Whose taste, too long forborne, at first assay

737 impregned. Impregnated.   *747. forborne.* Resisted.   *assay.* Attempt.

Gave elocution to the mute, and taught
The tongue not made for speech to speak thy praise:
Thy praise he also who forbids thy use,   750
Conceals not from us, naming thee the tree
Of knowledge, knowledge both of good and evil;
Forbids us then to taste, but his forbidding
Commends thee more, while it infers the good
By thee communicated, and our want: 755
For good unknown, sure is not had; or had
And yet unknown, is as not had at all.
In plain then, what forbids he but to know,
Forbids us good, forbids us to be wise?
Such prohibitions bind not. But if death   760
Bind us with after-bands, what profits then
Our inward freedom? In the day we eat
Of this fair fruit, our doom is, we shall die.
How dies the serpent? He hath eaten and lives,
And knows, and speaks, and reasons, and discerns,   765
Irrational till then. For us alone
Was death invented? Or to us denied
This intellectual food, for beasts reserved?
For beasts it seems: yet that one beast which first
Hath tasted, envies not, but brings with joy   770
The good befallen him, author unsuspect,
Friendly to man, far from deceit or guile.

761. *after-bands.* Later bonds. *771. author unsuspect.* Trustworthy informant.

What fear I then, rather what know to fear
Under this ignorance of good and evil,
Of god or death, of law or penalty?   775
Here grows the cure of all, this fruit divine,
Fair to the eye, inviting to the taste,
Of virtue to make wise: what hinders then
To reach, and feed at once both body and mind?
   So saying, her rash hand in evil hour   780
Forth reaching to the fruit, she plucked, she ate:
Earth felt the wound; and nature from her seat
Sighing through all her works gave signs of woe,
That all was lost. Back to the thicket slunk
The guilty serpent; and well might; for Eve,   785
Intent now wholly on her taste, nought else
Regarded; such delight till then, as seemed,
In fruit she never tasted, whether true
Or fancied so, through expectation high
Of knowledge; nor was godhead from her thought.   790
Greedily she engorged without restraint,
And knew not eating death: satiate at length,
And heightened as with wine, jocund and boon,
Thus to herself she pleasingly began.
   O sovereign, virtuous, precious of all trees   795
In Paradise! of operation blest
To sapience, hitherto obscured, infamed,

793. boon. Merry.   *797. sapience.* Wisdom   *infamed.* Defamed.

And thy fair fruit let hang, as to no end
Created; but henceforth my early care,
Not without song, each morning, and due praise   800
Shall tend thee, and the fertile burden ease
Of thy full branches offered free to all;
Till dieted by thee I grow mature
In knowledge, as the gods who all things know;
Though others envy what they cannot give;   805
For had the gift been theirs, it had not here
Thus grown. Experience, next to thee I owe,
Best guide; not following thee, I had remained
In ignorance; thou op'nest wisdom's way,
And giv'st access, though secret she retire.   810
And I perhaps am secret; heaven is high,
High and remote to see from thence distinct
Each thing on earth; and other care perhaps
May have diverted from continual watch
Our great forbidder, safe with all his spies   815
About him. But to Adam in what sort
Shall I appear? Shall I to him make known
As yet my change, and give him to partake
Full happiness with me, or rather not,
But keep the odds of knowledge in my power   820

805. others. Meaning God.   *807. Next to thee I owe.* I am indebted next (after the fruit)
to you. Eve addresses 'Experience', with connotations of experiment, courage and
risk-taking.   *815. forbidder.* God.

[171]

Without copartner? So to add what wants
In female sex, the more to draw his love,
And render me more equal, and perhaps,
A thing not undesirable, sometime
Superior; for inferior who is free?   825
This may be well: but what if God have seen,
And death ensue? Then I shall be no more,
And Adam wedded to another Eve,
Shall live with her enjoying, I extinct;
A death to think. Confirmed then I resolve,   830
Adam shall share with me in bliss or woe:
So dear I love him, that with him all deaths
I could endure, without him live no life.

     So saying, from the tree her step she turned,
But first low reverence done, as to the power   835
That dwelt within, whose presence had infused
Into the plant sciential sap, derived
From nectar, drink of gods. Adam the while,
Waiting desirous her return, had wove
Of choicest flowers a garland to adorn   840
Her tresses, and her rural labours crown
As reapers oft are wont their harvest queen.
Great joy he promised to his thoughts, and new
Solace in her return, so long delayed;
Yet oft his heart, divine of something ill,   845

---

837. sciential. Knowledge-giving.   *845. divine of.* With premonition of.

Misgave him; he the faltering measure felt;
And forth to meet her went, the way she took
That morn when first they parted: by the tree
Of knowledge he must pass; there he her met,
Scarce from the tree returning; in her hand   850
A bough of fairest fruit, that downy smiled,
New gathered, and ambrosial smell diffused.
To him she hasted; in her face excuse
Came prologue, and apology too prompt,
Which with bland words at will she thus addressed.   855
    Hast thou not wondered, Adam, at my stay?
Thee I have missed, and thought it long, deprived
Thy presence; agony of love till now
Not felt, nor shall be twice; for never more
Mean I to try, what rash untried I sought,   860
The pain of absence from thy sight. But strange
Hath been the cause, and wonderful to hear:
This tree is not as we are told, a tree
Of danger tasted, nor to evil unknown
Opening the way, but of divine effect   865
To open eyes, and make them gods who taste;
And hath been tasted such: the serpent wise,
Or not restrained as we, or not obeying,
Hath eaten of the fruit; and is become,

---

846. faltering measure. Of his heartbeats. *851. smiled.* Looked inviting. *868. Or . . . or.*
Either . . . or.

Not dead, as we are threatened, but thenceforth   870
Endued with human voice and human sense,
Reasoning to admiration; and with me
Persuasively hath so prevailed, that I
Have also tasted, and have also found
The effects to correspond; opener mine eyes,   875
Dim erst, dilated spirits, ampler heart,
And growing up to godhead; which for thee
Chiefly I sought, without thee can despise.
For bliss, as thou hast part, to me is bliss;
Tedious, unshared with thee, and odious soon.   880
Thou therefore also taste, that equal lot
May join us, equal joy, as equal love;
Lest thou not tasting, different degree
Disjoin us, and I then too late renounce
Deity for thee, when fate will not permit.   885
    Thus Eve with countenance blithe her story told;
But in her cheek distemper flushing glowed.
On the other side, Adam, soon as he heard
The fatal trespass done by Eve, amazed,
Astonied stood and blank, while horror chill   890
Ran through his veins, and all his joints relaxed;
From his slack hand the garland wreathed for Eve

872. *to admiration.* Admirably. 876. *erst.* Previously. 879. *as.* If. 885. *Deity.* The godly
status she imagines the fruit has conferred. 887. *distemper.* Bodily disturbance.
890. *blank.* Stunned.

Down dropped, and all the faded roses shed:
Speechless he stood and pale, till thus at length
First to himself he inward silence broke.   895
 O fairest of creation, last and best
Of all God's works, creature in whom excelled
Whatever can to sight or thought be formed,
Holy, divine, good, amiable, or sweet!
How art thou lost, how on a sudden lost,   900
Defaced, deflowered, and now to death devote!
Rather how hast thou yielded to transgress
The strict forbiddance, how to violate
The sacred fruit forbidden! Some cursed fraud
Of enemy hath beguiled thee, yet unknown,   905
And me with thee hath ruined; for with thee
Certain my resolution is to die;
How can I live without thee, how forgo
Thy sweet converse and love so dearly joined,
To live again in these wild woods forlorn?   910
Should God create another Eve, and I
Another rib afford, yet loss of thee
Would never from my heart; no no, I feel
The link of nature draw me: flesh of flesh,
Bone of my bone thou art, and from thy state   915
Mine never shall be parted, bliss or woe.
 So having said, as one from sad dismay

893. and ... shed. Inversion. The garland shed the roses. *901. devote.* Destined.

Recomforted, and after thoughts disturbed
Submitting to what seemed remediless,
Thus in calm mood his words to Eve he turned.   920

    Bold deed thou hast presumed, adventurous Eve,
And peril great provoked, who thus hast dared
Had it been only coveting to eye
That sacred fruit, sacred to abstinence,
Much more to taste it under ban to touch.   925
But past who can recall, or done undo?
Not God omnipotent, nor fate; yet so
Perhaps thou shalt not die, perhaps the fact
Is not so heinous now, foretasted fruit,
Profaned first by the serpent, by him first   930
Made common and unhallowed ere our taste;
Nor yet on him found deadly, he yet lives,
Lives, as thou saidst, and gains to live as man
Higher degree of life, inducement strong
To us, as likely tasting to attain   935
Proportional ascent; which cannot be
But to be gods, or angels, demigods.
Nor can I think that God, creator wise,
Though threatening, will in earnest so destroy
Us his prime creatures, dignified so high,   940

---

919. seemed. Suggesting there was a remedy. Perhaps to beg mercy from God; perhaps, as some critics suggest, to divorce Eve as a faithless idolator in line with Milton's views on divorce. *924. sacred to abstinence.* To be resisted as a holy thing. *940. his prime creatures.* Not so. Angels were made first.

Set over all his works; which in our fall,
For us created, needs with us must fail,
Dependent made; so God shall uncreate,
Be frustrate, do, undo, and labour lose;
Not well conceived of God, who though his power   945
Creation could repeat, yet would be loath
Us to abolish, lest the adversary
Triumph and say; Fickle their state whom God
Most favours; who can please him long? Me first
He ruined, now mankind; whom will he next?   950
Matter of scorn, not to be given the foe.
However I with thee have fixed my lot,
Certain to undergo like doom, if death
Consort with thee, death is to me as life;
So forcible within my heart I feel   955
The bond of nature draw me to my own,
My own in thee, for what thou art is mine;
Our state cannot be severed, we are one,
One flesh; to lose thee were to lose myself.

    So Adam; and thus Eve to him replied.   950
Oh glorious trial of exceeding love,
Illustrious evidence, example high!
Engaging me to emulate; but short
Of thy perfection, how shall I attain,

---

951. Matter . . . the foe. An opportunity for derision that should not be handed to an
enemy.

Adam, from whose dear side I boast me sprung,   965
And gladly of our union hear thee speak,
One heart, one soul in both; whereof good proof
This day affords, declaring thee resolved,
Rather than death or aught than death more dread
Shall separate us, linked in love so dear,   970
To undergo with me one guilt, one crime,
If any be, of tasting this fair fruit,
Whose virtue, for of good still good proceeds,
Direct, or by occasion hath presented
This happy trial of thy love, which else   975
So eminently never had been known.
Were it I thought death menaced would ensue
This my attempt, I would sustain alone
The worst, and not persuade thee, rather die
Deserted, than oblige thee with a fact   980
Pernicious to thy peace; chiefly assured ˙
Remarkably so late of thy so true,
So faithful love unequalled; but I feel
Far otherwise the event; not death, but life
Augmented, opened eyes, new hopes, new joys,   985
Taste so divine, that what of sweet before
Hath touched my sense, flat seems to this, and harsh.

973. *still.* Always.   974. *Direct ... occasion.* Directly or indirectly.   980. *oblige ...*
fact. Link you to a deed.   981. *chiefly assured.* Especially as I have proof.   984. *event.*
Outcome.

On my experience, Adam, freely taste,
And fear of death deliver to the winds.
  So saying, she embraced him, and for joy   990
Tenderly wept; much won that he his love
Had so ennobled, as of choice to incur
Divine displeasure for her sake, or death.
In recompense (for such compliance bad
Such recompense best merits) from the bough   995
She gave him of that fair enticing fruit
With liberal hand: he scrupled not to eat,
Against his better knowledge; not deceived,
But fondly overcome with female charm.
Earth trembled from her entrails, as again   1000
In pangs; and nature gave a second groan;
Sky loured; and, muttering thunder, some sad drops
Wept at completing of the mortal sin
Original; while Adam took no thought,
Eating his fill, nor Eve to iterate   1005
Her former trespass feared, the more to soothe
Him with her loved society; that now
As with new wine intoxicated both,
They swim in mirth, and fancy that they feel
Divinity within them breeding wings   1010
Wherewith to scorn the earth: but that false fruit

999. fondly. Foolishly.

Far other operation first displayed,
Carnal desire inflaming; he on Eve
Began to cast lascivious eyes; she him
As wantonly repaid; in lust they burn: 1015
Till Adam thus gan Eve to dalliance move.
    Eve, now I see thou art exact of taste,
And elegant, of sapience no small part;
Since to each meaning savour we apply,
And palate call judicious; I the praise   1020
Yield thee, so well this day thou hast purveyed.
Much pleasure we have lost, while we abstained
From this delightful fruit, nor known till now
True relish, tasting; if such pleasure be
In things to us forbidden, it might be wished,   1025
For this one tree had been forbidden ten.
But come, so well refreshed, now let us play,
As meet is, after such delicious fare;
For never did thy beauty since the day
I saw thee first and wedded thee, adorned   1030
With all perfections, so inflame my sense
With ardour to enjoy thee, fairer now
Than ever; bounty of this virtuous tree.
    So said he, and forbore not glance or toy

1018. *sapience.* (1) taste, (2) intelligence. Adam's punning is the first sign he is
fallen.   *1019.* In the seventeenth century 'savour' could mean both tastiness and
understanding.   *1021. purveyed.* Provided.

Of amorous intent; well understood   1035
Of Eve, whose eye darted contagious fire.
Her hand he seized; and to a shady bank,
Thick overhead with verdant roof embowered
He led her nothing loath; flowers were the couch,
Pansies, and violets, and asphodel,   1040
And hyacinth, earth's freshest softest lap.
There they their fill of love and love's disport
Took largely, of their mutual guilt the seal,
The solace of their sin, till dewy sleep
Oppressed them, wearied with their amorous play.   1045
Soon as the force of that fallacious fruit,
That with exhilarating vapour bland
About their spirits had played, and inmost powers
Made err, was now exhaled; and grosser sleep,
Bred of unkindly fumes, with conscious dreams   1050
Encumbered, now had left them; up they rose
As from unrest, and each the other viewing,
Soon found their eyes how opened, and their minds
How darkened; innocence, that as a veil
Had shadowed them from knowing ill, was gone,   1055
Just confidence, and native righteousness,
And honour from about them, naked left
To guilty shame; he covered, but his robe

1049. exhaled. Exhausted. *1050. unkindly.* Unnatural. *conscious.* Guilty. *1058. he.*
Shame, echoing Psalm 109:29, 'clothed with shame'.

Uncovered more. So rose the Danite strong
Herculean Samson from the harlot-lap   1060
Of Philistean Dalilah, and waked
Shorn of his strength, they destitute and bare
Of all their virtue: silent, and in face
Confounded long they sat, as strucken mute,
Till Adam, though not less than Eve abashed,   1065
At length gave utterance to these words constrained.
    O Eve, in evil hour thou didst give ear
To that false worm, of whomsoever taught
To counterfeit man's voice; true in our fall,
False in our promised rising; since our eyes   1070
Opened we find indeed, and find we know
Both good and evil, good lost, and evil got,
Bad fruit of knowledge, if this be to know,
Which leaves us naked thus, of honour void,
Of innocence, of faith, of purity,   1075
Our wonted ornaments now soiled and stained,
And in our faces evident the signs
Of foul concupiscence; whence evil store;
Even shame, the last of evils; of the first
Be sure then. How shall I behold the face   1080
Henceforth of God or angel, erst with joy
And rapture so oft beheld? Those heavenly shapes

1059–62. The Samson story is in Judges 16. *1067. Eve . . . evils.* Another pun.
1078. store. Manifold.

Will dazzle now this earthly, with their blaze
Insufferably bright. Oh might I here
In solitude live savage, in some glade   1085
Obscured, where highest woods, impenetrable
To star or sunlight, spread their umbrage broad
And brown as evening: cover me ye pines,
Ye cedars, with innumerable boughs
Hide me, where I may never see them more.   1090
But let us now, as in bad plight, devise
What best may for the present serve to hide
The parts of each from other, that seem most
To shame obnoxious, and unseemliest seen,
Some tree whose broad smooth leaves together sewed,   1095
And girded on our loins, may cover round
Those middle parts; that this newcomer, shame,
There sit not, and reproach us as unclean.
      So counselled he, and both together went
Into the thickest wood, there soon they chose   1100
The fig-tree, not that kind for fruit renowned,
But such as at this day, to Indians known
In Malabar or Decan spreads her arms
Branching so broad and long, that in the ground
The bended twigs take root and daughters grow   1105
About the mother tree, a pillared shade

1103–10. Malabar and the Deccan plateau are in southern India. Milton follows
seventeenth-century accounts of the banyan or Indian fig.

High overarched, and echoing walks between;
There oft the Indian herdsman shunning heat,
Shelters in cool, and tends his pasturing herds
At loopholes cut through thickest shade: those leaves   1110
They gathered, broad as Amazonian targe;
And with what skill they had, together sewed,
To gird their waist, vain covering if to hide
Their guilt and dreaded shame; oh how unlike
To that first naked glory. Such of late   1115
Columbus found the American so girt
With feathered cincture, naked else and wild
Among the trees on isles and woody shores.
Thus fenced, and as they thought, their shame in part
Covered, but not at rest or ease of mind,   1120
They sat them down to weep; nor only tears
Rained at their eyes, but high winds worse within
Began to rise, high passions, anger, hate,
Mistrust, suspicion, discord; and shook sore
Their inward state of mind, calm region once   1125
And full of peace, now tossed and turbulent:
For understanding ruled not, and the will
Heard not her lore, both in subjection now
To sensual appetite, who from beneath
Usurping over sovereign reason claimed   1130

1111. *Amazonian targe.* Shield of an Amazon, legendary woman warrior. *1116.*
Columbus had first reached America in 1492. *1118. cincture.* Belt.

Superior sway: from thus distempered breast,
Adam, estranged in look and altered style,
Speech intermitted thus to Eve renewed.

   Would thou hadst hearkened to my words, and stayed
With me, as I besought thee, when that strange   1135
Desire of wandering this unhappy morn,
I know not whence possessed thee; we had then
Remained still happy, not as now, despoiled
Of all our good; shamed, naked, miserable.
Let none henceforth seek needless cause to approve   1140
The faith they owe; when earnestly they seek
Such proof, conclude, they then begin to fail.

   To whom soon moved with touch of blame thus Eve.
What words have passed thy lips, Adam severe,
Imput'st thou that to my default, or will   1145
Of wandering, as thou callst it, which who knows
But might as ill have happened thou being by,
Or to thyself perhaps: hadst thou been there,
Or here the attempt, thou couldst not have discerned
Fraud in the serpent, speaking as he spake;   1150
No ground of enmity between us known,
Why he should mean me ill, or seek to harm.
Was I to have never parted from thy side?
As good have grown there still a lifeless rib.

1132. style. Way of talking. *1140–1. Seek needless cause . . . owe.* As Eve had in gardening
alone.

Being as I am, why didst not thou the head   1155
Command me absolutely not to go,
Going into such danger as thou saidst?
Too facile then thou didst not much gainsay;
Nay, didst permit, approve, and fair dismiss.
Hadst thou been firm and fixed in thy dissent,   1160
Neither had I transgressed, nor thou with me.
   To whom then first incensed Adam replied.
Is this the love, is this the recompense
Of mine to thee, ingrateful Eve, expressed
Immutable when thou wert lost, not I,   1165
Who might have lived and joyed immortal bliss,
Yet willingly chose rather death with thee:
And am I now upbraided, as the cause
Of thy transgressing? Not enough severe,
It seems, in thy restraint: what could I more?   1170
I warned thee, I admonished thee, foretold
The danger, and the lurking enemy
That lay in wait; beyond this had been force;
And force upon free will hath here no place.
But confidence then bore thee on, secure   1175
Either to meet no danger, or to find
Matter of glorious trial; and perhaps
I also erred in overmuch admiring

1158. *gainsay.* Oppose. *1164. mine.* My love. *1169. Not enough severe.* Picking up Eve's
accusation in lines 1155–6.

What seemed in thee so perfect, that I thought
No evil durst attempt thee, but I rue   1180
The error now, which is become my crime,
And thou the accuser. Thus it shall befall
Him who to worth in women overtrusting
Lets her will rule; restraint she will not brook,
And left to herself, if evil thence ensue,   1185
She first his weak indulgence will accuse.

   Thus they in mutual accusation spent
The fruitless hours, but neither self-condemning,
And of their vain contest appeared no end.

1184. *brook.* Tolerate.

BOOK 10

News of Adam and Eve's fall reaches heaven. The angels assemble, and the Father addresses them from his 'secret cloud'. He tells them he has 'transferred/All judgement' to his 'Vicegerent Son' and will send him to judge fallen man. The Son replies that as he is to die for fallen mankind he has the right to 'mitigate their doom', and will temper 'justice with mercy'. All the angelic orders accompany him to heaven's gate, and he swiftly descends to earth.

Now was the sun in western cadence low
From noon, and gentle airs, due at their hour,
To fan the earth now waked, and usher in
The evening cool when he from wrath more cool,   95
Came the mild judge and Intercessor both
To sentence man; the voice of God they heard
Now walking in the garden, by soft winds
Brought to their ears, while day declined, they heard,
And from his presence hid themselves among   100
The thickest trees, both man and wife; till God
Approaching, thus to Adam called aloud.
    Where art thou, Adam, wont with joy to meet

92. cadence. Descent.

My coming seen far off? I miss thee here,
Not pleased, thus entertained with solitude,   105
Where obvious duty erewhile appeared unsought:
Or come I less conspicuous, or what change
Absents thee, or what chance detains? Come forth.
He came, and with him Eve, more loath, though first
To offend, discount'nanced both, and discomposed;   110
Love was not in their looks, either to God,
Or to each other; but apparent guilt,
And shame, and perturbation, and despair,
Anger, and obstinacy, and hate, and guile.
Whence Adam faltering long, thus answered brief.   115
    I heard thee in the garden, and of thy voice
Afraid, being naked, hid myself. To whom
The gracious judge without revile replied.
    My voice thou oft hast heard, and hast not feared,
But still rejoiced, how is it now become   120
So dreadful to thee? That thou art naked, who
Hath told thee? Hast thou eaten of the tree
Whereof I gave thee charge thou shouldst not eat?
    To whom thus Adam sore beset replied.
O heaven! In evil strait this day I stand   125
Before my judge; either to undergo
Myself the total crime, or to accuse
My other self, the partner of my life;

---

106. *obvious.* (1) clear (2) related to a meeting of ways. *118. revile.* Recrimination.
120. still. Always.

Whose failing, while her faith to me remains,
I should conceal, and not expose to blame   130
By my complaint; but strict necessity
Subdues me, and calamitous constraint,
Lest on my head both sin and punishment,
However insupportable, be all
Devolved; though should I hold my peace, yet thou   135
Wouldst easily detect what I conceal.
This woman whom thou mad'st to be my help,
And gav'st me as thy perfect gift, so good,
So fit, so acceptable, so divine,
That from her hand I could suspect no ill,   140
And what she did, whatever in itself,
Her doing seemed to justify the deed;
She gave me of the tree, and I did eat.
    To whom the sovereign presence thus replied.
Was she thy God, that her thou didst obey   145
Before his voice, or was she made thy guide,
Superior, or but equal, that to her
Thou didst resign thy manhood, and the place
Wherein God set thee above her made of thee,
And for thee, whose perfection far excelled   150
Hers in all real dignity; adorned
She was indeed, and lovely to attract
Thy love, not thy subjection, and her gifts

---

140. That . . . ill. A lie. Adam fell knowingly.

Were such as under government well seemed,
Unseemly to bear rule, which was thy part   155
And person, hadst thou known thyself aright.
   So having said, he thus to Eve in few:
Say woman, what is this which thou hast done?
   To whom sad Eve with shame nigh overwhelmed,
Confessing soon, yet not before her judge   160
Bold or loquacious, thus abashed replied.
   The serpent me beguiled and I did eat.

The penalties that God announces match those in the Genesis account of the fall. The serpent is cursed: it will go on its belly and eat dust. Eve's seed will bruise the serpent's head – a prophecy, Milton points out, of Christ's eventual triumph over Satan after his Second Coming. Eve will give birth to children in sorrow and be subject to her husband's will. The earth will be cursed and bring forth thorns and thistles, and Adam will eat bread in the sweat of his face. Pitying Adam and Eve's nakedness, the Son clothes them in animal skins before departing.

Sin and Death build a causeway linking the earth to hell. Meeting Satan, they glory in the vengeance he has taken on God. He returns to hell and tells the assembled devils of his triumph. But when he expects their applause, he and all the other devils find themselves changed to serpents, chewing bitter ashes and filling hell with hisses. This is a temporary change, but 'some say', Milton writes, that the devils are turned to snakes for a certain number of days each year, to 'dash their pride'.

155. Unseemly. Unsuitable.

*God looks down from heaven and points out the activities of Sin
and Death to the heavenly host.*

See with what heat these dogs of hell advance
To waste and havoc yonder world, which I
So fair and good created, and had still
Kept in that state, had not the folly of man
Let in these wasteful furies, who impute   620
Folly to me; so doth the prince of hell
And his adherents, that with so much ease
I suffer them to enter and possess
A place so heavenly; and, conniving, seem
To gratify my scornful enemies,   625
That laugh, as if transported with some fit
Of passion, I to them had quitted all,
At random yielded up to their misrule;
And know not that I called and drew them thither,
My hell-hounds, to lick up the draff and filth   630
Which man's polluting sin with taint hath shed
On what was pure; till crammed and gorged, nigh burst
With sucked and glutted offal, at one sling
Of thy victorious arm, well-pleasing Son,
Both Sin and Death, and yawning grave, at last,   635
Through chaos hurled, obstruct the mouth of hell
For ever, and seal up his ravenous jaws.

630. draff. Garbage.

Then heaven and earth renewed shall be made pure
To sanctity that shall receive no stain:
Till then, the curse pronounced on both precedes.   640

The heavenly host praise God's justice.
     *God meanwhile makes some meteorological adjustments as part of
man's punishment. He sends angels to alter the relative motions and
positions of the sun, earth and planets so that the earth suffers 'scarce
tolerable' cold and heat and the stars send down 'malignant' influence.
The new phenomenon of seasonal weather-change replaces what had
been the perpetual spring of Eden. The peace of Paradise is replaced by
a proto-Darwinian battle for survival.*

Beast now with beast gan war, and fowl with fowl,   710
And fish with fish; to graze the herb all leaving,
Devoured each other; nor stood much in awe
Of man, but fled him; or with countenance grim
Glared on him passing: these were from without
The growing miseries, which Adam saw   715
Already in part, though hid in gloomiest shade,
To sorrow abandoned, but worse felt within.
And in a troubled sea of passion tossed,
Thus to disburden sought with sad complaint.
     Oh miserable of happy! Is this the end   720
Of this new glorious world, and me so late

640. *both.* Heaven and earth. *precedes.* Comes before their renewal. *710. gan.* Began.

The glory of that glory, who now become
Accursed of blessed, hide me from the face
Of God, whom to behold was then my height
Of happiness: yet well, if here would end   725
The misery, I deserved it, and would bear
My own deservings; but this will not serve;
All that I eat or drink, or shall beget,
Is propagated curse. Oh voice once heard
Delightfully, *Increase and multiply*,   730
Now death to hear! For what can I increase
Or multiply, but curses on my head?
Who of all ages to succeed, but feeling
The evil on him brought by me, will curse
My head: *Ill fare our ancestor impure,*   735
For this we may thank Adam! But his thanks
Shall be the execration: so besides
Mine own that bide upon me, all from me
Shall with a fierce reflux on me rebound,
On me as on their natural centre light   740
Heavy, though in their place. Oh fleeting joys
Of Paradise, dear bought with lasting woes!
Did I request thee, Maker, from my clay
To mould me man, did I solicit thee
From darkness to promote me, or here place   745

723. of. Instead of. *737. execration.* The curse in the two previous lines. *738. Mine*
own. My own curses (referring back to line 732).

In this delicious garden? As my will
Concurred not to my being, it were but right
And equal to reduce me to my dust,
Desirous to resign, and render back
All I received, unable to perform   750
Thy terms too hard, by which I was to hold
The good I sought not. To the loss of that,
Sufficient penalty, why hast thou added
The sense of endless woes? Inexplicable
Thy justice seems; yet to say truth, too late   755
I thus contest; then should have been refused
Those terms whatever, when they were proposed:
Thou didst accept them; wilt thou enjoy the good,
Then cavil the conditions? And though God
Made thee without thy leave, what if thy son   760
Prove disobedient, and reproved, retort,
Wherefore didst thou beget me? I sought it not!
Wouldst thou admit for his contempt of thee
That proud excuse? Yet him not thy election,
But natural necessity begot.   765
God made thee of choice his own, and of his own
To serve him; thy reward was of his grace,
Thy punishment then justly is at his will.
Be it so, for I submit, his doom is fair,
That dust I am, and shall to dust return: 770

759. *cavil.* Question.   760–1. *What ... disobedient.* Echoing Isaiah 45:10.

Oh welcome hour whenever! Why delays
His hand to execute what his decree
Fixed on this day? Why do I overlive,
Why am I mocked with death, and lengthened out
To deathless pain? How gladly would I meet 775
Mortality my sentence, and be earth
Insensible, how glad would lay me down
As in my mother's lap! There I should rest
And sleep secure; his dreadful voice no more
Would thunder in my ears; no fear of worse 780
To me and to my offspring would torment me
With cruel expectation. Yet one doubt
Pursues me still, lest all I cannot die,
Lest that pure breath of life, the spirit of man
Which God inspired, cannot together perish 785
With this corporeal clod; then in the grave,
Or in some other dismal place, who knows
But I shall die a living death? Oh thought
Horrid, if true! Yet why? It was but breath
Of life that sinned; what dies but what had life 790
And sin? The body properly had neither.
All of me then shall die: let this appease
The doubt, since human reach no further knows.
For though the Lord of all be infinite,

772–3. decree . . . this day. Adam misremembers. God's decree was not that he would
die that day, but be 'From that day mortal', Book 8:330–2.

Is his wrath also? Be it, man is not so,   795
But mortal doomed. How can he exercise
Wrath without end on man whom death must end?
Can he make deathless death? That were to make
Strange contradiction, which to God himself
Impossible is held; as argument   800
Of weakness, not of power. Will he draw out,
For anger's sake, finite to infinite
In punished man, to satisfy his rigour,
Satisfied never? That were to extend
His sentence beyond dust and nature's law,   805
By which all causes else according still
To the reception of their matter act,
Not to the extent of their own sphere. But say
That death be not one stroke, as I supposed,
Bereaving sense, but endless misery   810
From this day onward, which I feel begun
Both in me, and without me, and so last
To perpetuity? Ay me, that fear
Comes thundering back with dreadful revolution
On my defenceless head; both death and I   815
Am found eternal, and incorporate both,
Nor I on my part single, in me all

806–8. *By which . . . sphere.* That agents act according to the receiving-capacity of their
subjects was an Aristotelian doctrine.   *812. Without.* Outside.   *816. incorporate.* United
in one body.   *817. Nor . . . single.* Because all my descendants must die too.

Posterity stands cursed: fair patrimony
That I must leave ye, sons, oh were I able
To waste it all myself, and leave ye none!   820
So disinherited how would ye bless
Me, now your curse! Ah, why should all mankind,
For one man's fault, thus guiltless be condemned,
If guiltless? But from me what can proceed,
But all corrupt, both mind and will depraved,   825
Not to do only, but to will the same
With me? How can they then acquitted stand
In sight of God? Him after all disputes
Forced I absolve: all my evasions vain
And reasonings, though through mazes, lead me still   830
But to my own conviction: first and last
On me, me only, as the source and spring
Of all corruption, all the blame lights due;
So might the wrath! Fond wish! Couldst thou support
That burden heavier than the earth to bear,   835
Than all the world much heavier, though divided
With that bad woman? Thus what thou desir'st,
And what thou fearst, alike destroys all hope
Of refuge and concludes thee miserable
Beyond all past example and future;   840
To Satan only like both crime and doom.
O conscience, into what abyss of fears

---

820. *waste*. Expend the 'patrimony'.

And horrors hast thou driven me; out of which
I find no way, from deep to deeper plunged!

This soliloquy by Adam (720–844) is as close as Paradise Lost *comes to making out a case against God's justice. Adam's protest that he did not ask to be created (743–52) is reasonable, and it makes no sense to say he should have refused the 'terms' when they were proposed (755–6), since by that time he had already been created.*

The comparison with human fathers (759–66) works out to God's disadvantage. As Adam points out, God created man as a matter of choice, not driven by a natural urge as human fathers are. Therefore God is entirely responsible for bringing man into being, as a human father is not.

Christians believe, as Milton did, that God made man immortal and able to suffer in hell for all eternity. Adam, it now becomes clear, had not realised this, and God did not make any effort to explain to him what the death sentence for eating the fruit really meant. Adam's suspicion, 'Horrid, if true!' (789), is true, though horrid. By making humans immortal God does, Christians believe, 'make deathless death', and draw out 'finite to infinite' in man. For those humans who would be numbered among the damned (the majority, as most seventeenth-century Christians believed) the effect of immortality would be to ensure eternal punishment – 'to satisfy his rigour,/Satisfied never' (798–808).

Milton had a keen critical intelligence. He was adept, in his political writing, at picking to pieces other people's arguments. It is hard to believe that he did not see the strength of Adam's complaints and the weakness of his attempts to justify God.

Why he let this soliloquy remain as part of his poem is hard to explain. Possibly he thought that the true Christian must learn to confront these arguments against God's justice, and learn, despite them, to trust implicitly in God's goodness. Alternatively we may read them as expressing Milton's own doubts.

That Adam's questionings correspond closely to Milton's own can be demonstrated with respect to at least one of the subjects Adam covers – his argument that the soul must die with the body (789–93). In Christian Doctrine *Milton uses reasoning similar to Adam's to conclude that the soul and body die together (a heresy known as Mortalism in the seventeenth century). However, the soul would, Milton believed, be resurrected at the Last Judgement, so the 'strange contradiction' of God making 'deathless death' (798–9), which so horrifies Adam, remains.*

Thus Adam to himself lamented loud   845
Through the still night, not now, as ere man fell,
Wholesome and cool and mild, but with black air
Accompanied, with damps and dreadful gloom,
Which to his evil conscience represented
All things with double terror: on the ground   850
Outstretched he lay, on the cold ground, and oft
Cursed his creation, death as oft accused
Of tardy execution, since denounced
The day of his offence. Why comes not death,
Said he, with one thrice-acceptable stroke   855
To end me? Shall truth fail to keep her word,
Justice divine not hasten to be just?

But death comes not at call, justice divine
Mends not her slowest pace for prayers or cries.
O woods, O fountains, hillocks, dales, and bowers,   860
With other echo late I taught your shades
To answer, and resound far other song.
Whom thus afflicted when sad Eve beheld,
Desolate where she sat, approaching nigh,
Soft words to his fierce passion she assayed: 865
But her with stern regard he thus repelled.

   Out of my sight, thou serpent, that name best
Befits thee with him leagued, thyself as false
And hateful; nothing wants, but that thy shape,
Like his, and colour serpentine may show   870
Thy inward fraud, to warn all creatures from thee
Henceforth; lest that too heavenly form, pretended
To hellish falsehood, snare them. But for thee
I had persisted happy, had not thy pride
And wandering vanity, when least was safe,   875
Rejected my forewarning, and disdained
Not to be trusted; longing to be seen
Though by the devil himself, him overweening
To overreach, but with the serpent meeting
Fooled and beguiled, by him thou, I by thee,   880

---

863. *Whom . . . beheld.* Latinate word order. 'When sad Eve beheld him thus afflicted'.
869. *wants.* Is lacking.   872. *pretended.* Providing a cover to.   878–9. *overweening . . .*
overreach. Foolishly believing you could get the better of.

To trust thee from my side; imagined wise,
Constant, mature, proof against all assaults,
And understood not all was but a show,
Rather than solid virtue, all but a rib
Crooked by nature, bent, as now appears,   885
More to the part sinister from me drawn;
Well if thrown out, as supernumerary
To my just number found. Oh why did God,
Creator wise, that peopled highest heaven
With spirits masculine, create at last   890
This novelty on earth, this fair defect
Of nature, and not fill the world at once
With men as angels without feminine;
Or find some other way to generate
Mankind? This mischief had not then befallen,   895
And more that shall befall; innumerable
Disturbances on earth through female snares,
And strait conjunction with this sex: for either
He never shall find out fit mate, but such
As some misfortune brings him, or mistake;   900
Or whom he wishes most shall seldom gain

---

881. imagined. [Whom I] imagined. *886. sinister.* (1) left (2) evil. *887. supernumerary.*
Unnecessary. *888. just.* Correct. *890. With spirits masculine.* In fact angels could
'either sex assume, or both', Book 1:424, but Adam has heard only of male angels.
898. strait. Close. *899. He.* Man, in future. *901. whom . . . gain.* Inversion. Shall
seldom gain whom he wishes most.

Through her perverseness, but shall see her gained
By a far worse, or if she love, withheld
By parents, or his happiest choice too late
Shall meet, already linked and wedlock-bound   905
To a fell adversary, his hate or shame:
Which infinite calamity shall cause
To human life, and household peace confound.

    He added not, and from her turned, but Eve
Not so repulsed, with tears that ceased not flowing,   910
And tresses all disordered, at his feet
Fell humble; and embracing them, besought
His peace, and thus proceeded in her plaint.

    Forsake me not thus, Adam, witness heaven
What love sincere, and reverence in my heart   915
I bear thee, and unweeting have offended,
Unhappily deceived; thy suppliant
I beg, and clasp thy knees; bereave me not,
Whereon I live, thy gentle looks, thy aid,
Thy counsel in this uttermost distress,   920
My only strength and stay: forlorn of thee,
Whither shall I betake me, where subsist?
While yet we live, scarce one short hour perhaps,
Between us two let there be peace, both joining,
As joined in injuries, one enmity   925
Against a foe by doom express assigned us,

916. *unweeting.* Unknowing.   918. *bereave.* Deprive of.

That cruel serpent: on me exercise not
Thy hatred for this misery befallen,
On me already lost, me than thyself
More miserable: both have sinned; but thou   930
Against God only, I against God and thee,
And to the place of judgement will return,
There with my cries importune heaven, that all
The sentence from thy head removed, may light
On me, sole cause to thee of all this woe;   935
Me, me only just object of his ire.

   She ended weeping, and her lowly plight,
Immoveable till peace obtained from fault
Acknowledged and deplored, in Adam wrought
Commiseration; soon his heart relented   940
Towards her, his life so late and sole delight,
Now at his feet submissive in distress,
Creature so fair his reconcilement seeking,
His counsel, whom she had displeased, his aid;
As one disarmed, his anger all he lost,   945
And thus with peaceful words upraised her soon.

   Unwary, and too desirous, as before,
So now of what thou know'st not, who desir'st
The punishment all on thyself, alas,
Bear thine own first, ill able to sustain   950
His full wrath whose thou feelst as yet least part,

---

938. till . . . obtained. Till she obtained peace. *941. late.* Recently.

And my displeasure bearst so ill. If prayers
Could alter high decrees, I to that place
Would speed before thee, and be louder heard,
That on my head all might be visited,   955
Thy frailty and infirmer sex forgiven,
To me committed and by me exposed.
But rise, let us no more contend, nor blame
Each other, blamed enough elsewhere, but strive
In offices of love, how we may light'n   960
Each other's burden in our share of woe;
Since this day's death denounced, if aught I see,
Will prove no sudden, but a slow-paced evil,
A long day's dying to augment our pain,
And to our seed (oh hapless seed!) derived.   965

Eve suggests that they should refrain from having children or, if chas-
tity seems too difficult, that they should commit suicide. This would end
their present suffering and prevent them generating a race of beings
doomed to death. Adam, though, is not persuaded.

Eve, thy contempt of life and pleasure seems
To argue in thee something more sublime
And excellent than what thy mind contemns;   1015
But self-destruction therefore sought, refutes

952–7. Compare Adam's terror when he could have taken full blame, Book 10:133–5.
965. seed. Descendants.

That excellence thought in thee; and implies,
Not thy contempt, but anguish and regret
For loss of life and pleasure overloved.
Or if thou covet death, as utmost end   1020
Of misery, so thinking to evade
The penalty pronounced, doubt not but God
Hath wiselier armed his vengeful ire, than so
To be forestalled; much more I fear lest death
So snatched will not exempt us from the pain   1025
We are by doom to pay; rather such acts
Of contumacy will provoke the highest
To make death in us live: then let us seek
Some safer resolution, which methinks
I have in view, calling to mind with heed   1030
Part of our sentence, that thy seed shall bruise
The serpent's head; piteous amends, unless
Be meant, whom I conjecture, our grand foe,
Satan; who in the serpent hath contrived
Against us this deceit: to crush his head   1035
Would be revenge indeed; which will be lost
By death brought on ourselves, or childless days
Resolved, as thou proposest; so our foe
Shall scape his punishment ordained, and we
Instead shall double ours upon our heads.   1040
No more be mentioned then of violence

1019. overloved. Loved too much.

Against ourselves; and wilful barrenness,
That cuts us off from hope; and savours only
Rancour and pride, impatience and despite,
Reluctance against God and his just yoke   1045
Laid on our necks. Remember with what mild
And gracious temper he both heard, and judged,
Without wrath or reviling; we expected
Immediate dissolution, which we thought
Was meant by death that day, when lo, to thee   1050
Pains only in child-bearing were foretold,
And bringing forth, soon recompensed with joy,
Fruit of thy womb: on me the curse aslope
Glanced on the ground, with labour I must earn
My bread; what harm? Idleness had been worse;   1055
My labour will sustain me; and lest cold
Or heat should injure us, his timely care
Hath unbesought provided, and his hands
Clothed us unworthy, pitying while he judged;
How much more, if we pray him, will his ear   1060
Be open, and his heart to pity incline,
And teach us further by what means to shun
The inclement seasons, rain, ice, hail, and snow,
Which now the sky with various face begins
To show us in this mountain; while the winds   1065
Blow moist and keen, shattering the graceful locks

1053–4. *aslope . . . ground.* Was deflected onto the earth, which was cursed.

Of these fair spreading trees; which bids us seek
Some better shroud, some better warmth to cherish
Our limbs benumbed, ere this diurnal star
Leave cold the night, how we his gathered beams   1070
Reflected, may with matter sere foment,
Or by collision of two bodies grind
The air attrite to fire; as late the clouds
Jostling or pushed with winds rude in their shock,
Tine the slant lightning; whose thwart flame, driv'n down   1075
Kindles the gummy bark of fir or pine;
And sends a comfortable heat from far,
Which might supply the sun: such fire to use,
And what may else be remedy or cure
To evils which our own misdeeds have wrought,   1080
He will instruct us praying, and of grace
Beseeching him, so as we need not fear
To pass commodiously this life, sustained
By him with many comforts, till we end
In dust, our final rest and native home.   1085
What better can we do, than to the place
Repairing where he judged us, prostrate fall
Before him reverent; and there confess

1068. *shroud*. Shelter.   1069. *diurnal star*. The sun.   1071. *sere*. Dry.   *foment*. Cherish.
1073. *attrite*. Subjected to friction.   *late*. Recently.   1075. *Tine*. Ignite.   *thwart*. Striking
crossways.   1078. *supply*. Take the place of.   1081. *us praying*. Us when we pray.   1087.
Repairing. Going.

Humbly our faults, and pardon beg, with tears
Watering the ground, and with our sighs the air   1090
Frequenting, sent from hearts contrite, in sign
Of sorrow unfeigned, and humiliation meek.
Undoubtedly he will relent, and turn
From his displeasure; in whose look serene,
When angry most he seemed and most severe,   1095
What else but favour, grace, and mercy, shone?
　So spake our father penitent, nor Eve
Felt less remorse: they forthwith to the place
Repairing where he judged them prostrate fell
Before him reverent, and both confessed   1100
Humbly their faults, and pardon begged; with tears
Watering the ground, and with their sighs the air
Frequenting, sent from hearts contrite, in sign
Of sorrow unfeigned, and humiliation meek.

1091. Frequenting. Filling.

BOOK 11

The Son presents Adam and Eve's prayers to the Father, and intercedes for them. The Father accepts their repentance, but he declares that they can no longer stay in Paradise. The reasons he gives are inconsistent. He tells the Son that Adam and Eve cannot stay in Paradise because natural law ('The law I gave to nature') forbids it. The garden's 'pure immortal elements' eject anything 'tainted', and this includes the human pair. However, he gives a different reason shortly afterwards to the assembled angels.

O sons, like one of us man is become
To know both good and evil, since his taste   85
Of that defended fruit; but let him boast
His knowledge of good lost, and evil got,
Happier, had it sufficed him to have known
Good by itself, and evil not at all.
He sorrows now, repents, and prays contrite,   90
My motions in him, longer than they move
His heart, I know how variable and vain
Self-left. Lest therefore his now bolder hand

---

86. defended. Forbidden. *91. My motions.* God claims credit, having given Adam grace to repent. *93. Self-left.* Left to himself.

Reach also of the tree of life, and eat,
And live for ever, dream at least to live   95
For ever, to remove him I decree,
And send him from the garden forth to till
The ground whence he was taken, fitter soil.

*God's words, 'dream at least to live/For ever', are Milton's addition to
the biblical account. In Genesis 3:22 God says that man must leave the
garden, 'lest he put forth his hand, and take also of the tree of life, and
eat, and live for ever'.*

*The God of Genesis is a primitive god with magic trees. In later
reinterpretations of Genesis, however, this primitive god was replaced
by something more theologically sophisticated. In* Paradise Lost *the
trees are not magic, just deceptively named. The human pair do not
really get knowledge of good and evil from the first tree – just drunk-
enness, lust and a hangover – and God implies that they will not really
live for ever if they eat fruit from the tree of life. But if that is so, there
seems no need to turn them out of the garden.*

*Whatever the reason, God sends Michael, with a guard of fiery
cherubim, to eject them. He also instructs Michael to tell Adam 'what
shall come in future days', adding that he will give Michael this infor-
mation so that he can pass it on.*

*When Michael reveals to the human pair that they must leave Par-
adise they are overcome with grief. However, he comforts them, and,
having put Eve to sleep, he takes Adam to a mountain top and gives
him a vision of mankind's future.*

He presents this as a catalogue of the evils that will result from

Adam's fall. But Michael's preview of mankind's history also takes the form of a series of false starts on God's part. God destroys his first creation, with the flood. But his second attempt turns out no better. So he abandons that, and concentrates on the Jews as his chosen people. However, they disappoint him too. So he sends his Son to replace the law that he gave to the Jews with a new dispensation of grace. Even under this dispensation a large number of human beings will be eternally damned.

Since God is all-knowing, he must have foreseen these disappointments. They cannot be regarded as mistakes, since an omniscient being cannot make mistakes. But why God chose such a devious path to reach the final point, when God will be 'all in all' (as foretold in I Corinthians 15:28, and repeated by Milton in Book 3:341), remains mysterious. Mysterious, too, is why he created mankind, or any other beings, if God being all in all is the ideal. Milton does not answer these questions, but the way he presents world history clearly raises them.

The visual show Michael lays on for Adam starts with the murder of Abel by Cain, then passes to a hospital where the patients suffer agonies from a wide range of physical and mental diseases. These are all caused, Michael assures Adam, by human intemperance in food and drink, and are traceable to Eve's eating of the apple. Adam weeps at the sight, but Michael tells him the sufferings are deserved since illness is caused by 'ungoverned appetite'.

The vision continues, showing the development of human technology, music and the arts of cultivated life. Adam is filled with admiration but Michael corrects him. Those he admires are 'atheists', he says, led astray by 'effeminate slackness' such as Adam displayed when he

was seduced by Eve. Visions of wars and battles follow, with Michael
condemning the false ideal of military glory. Then come scenes of lux-
ury and licentiousness, and Adam is shown Noah preaching conversion
and repentance in vain. Michael comments:

So all shall turn degenerate, all depraved,
Justice and temperance, truth and faith forgot;
One man except, the only son of light
In a dark age, against example, good,
Against allurement, custom, and a world   810
Offended; fearless of reproach and scorn,
Or violence, he of their wicked ways
Shall them admonish, and before them set
The paths of righteousness, how much more safe,
And full of peace; denouncing wrath to come   815
On their impenitence; and shall return
Of them derided, but of God observed
The one just man alive; by his command
Shall build a wondrous ark, as thou beheldst,
To save himself and household from amidst   820
A world devote to universal wreck.
No sooner he with them of man and beast
Select for life, shall in the ark be lodged,
And sheltered round but all the cataracts

808. *One man.* Noah.   819. *as thou beheldst.* In the visual show Michael has put on for
Adam.   821. *devote.* Destined.

Of heaven set open on the earth shall pour   825
Rain day and night, all fountains of the deep,
Broke up, shall heave the ocean to usurp
Beyond all bounds, till inundation rise
Above the highest hills: then shall this mount
Of Paradise by might of waves be moved   830
Out of his place, pushed by the horned flood,
With all his verdure spoiled, and trees adrift
Down the great river to the opening gulf,
And there take root an island salt and bare,
The haunt of seals and orcs, and seamews' clang.   835

The vision continues and shows the floods receding, the dove flying
from the ark and returning, Noah's family disembarking, and a rain-
bow appearing in heaven to signify, as Michael explains, God's cov-
enant that he will never again destroy the world by flood. Next time it
will be by fire, and will 'purge all things new', Michael adds.

---

831. horned. Imitating Virgil who calls the Tiber *corniger* (horned).   *835. clang.* Harsh
scream.

BOOK 12

Michael continues his narrative of the future, but now uses only words, without any visual aid. He tells of the building of the tower of Babel ('great laughter was in heaven') and the growth of tyranny (exemplified by Nimrod). Tyranny, he explains, is another punishment for the fall. Since Adam allowed 'upstart passions' to dominate his reason, God, 'in judgement just', subjects mankind to live under tyrannical regimes ('Though to the tyrant thereby no excuse'). So the human race will go from bad to worse, Michael foretells, and God will avert his 'holy eyes' from its 'polluted ways'. Withdrawing his presence from them, he will select Abraham and his descendants as his chosen people, from whom the redeemer will spring.

As a lead-up to the coming of Christ, Michael outlines early Jewish history – the captivity in Egypt, the plagues, the exodus, the giving of the ten commandments and the entrance to the promised land. Adam asks about the commandments, and Michael tells him that God always intended them as a temporary measure. They are 'imperfect', and will be replaced by the 'new covenant' embodied in Jesus.

Michael omits most of the events of Christ's earthly life, perhaps because they would be out of keeping with epic grandeur. The crucifixion is related in a single phrase – 'nailed to the cross' – which is quickly followed by a line in which Christ becomes the crucifier: 'But to the cross he nails thy enemies'. Christ's death is, Michael pointedly notes,

Adam's fault. He will die 'the death thou shouldst have died'. This seems questionable, since Adam will die and the Son of God will not, as Michael goes on to relate. Christ will, he explains, rise from death and, after his resurrection, instruct his disciples to preach the gospel to all nations, not just the Jews.

Then to the heaven of heavens he shall ascend
With victory, triumphing through the air
Over his foes and thine; there shall surprise
The serpent, prince of air, and drag in chains
Through all his realm, and there confounded leave;   455
Then enter into glory, and resume
His seat at God's right hand, exalted high
Above all names in heaven; and thence shall come,
When this world's dissolution shall be ripe,
With glory and power to judge both quick and dead,   460
To judge the unfaithful dead, but to reward
His faithful, and receive them into bliss,
Whether in heaven or earth, for then the earth
Shall all be Paradise, far happier place
Than this of Eden, and far happier days.   465
    So spake the archangel Michael, then paused,
As at the world's great period; and our sire

454. *drag in chains.* Based on 2 Peter 2:4: 'God spared not the angels that sinned but cast them down to hell and delivered them into chains of darkness to be reserved unto judgement'. 459. *dissolution.* Destruction. 467. *great period.* Major turning-point.

Replete with joy and wonder thus replied.

    Oh goodness infinite, goodness immense!

That all this good of evil shall produce,   470

And evil turn to good; more wonderful

Than that which by creation first brought forth

Light out of darkness! Full of doubt I stand,

Whether I should repent me now of sin

By me done and occasioned; or rejoice   475

Much more, that much more good thereof shall spring,

To God more glory, more good will to men

From God, and over wrath grace shall abound.

Adam asks what will happen to the disciples after Jesus's ascension, and Michael gives a brief history of the early church with its persecutions and martyrdoms. Without actually mentioning Roman Catholicism, he details the many iniquities of the Catholic church, as seen from a Protestant perspective. Adam is duly grateful.

Greatly instructed I shall hence depart,

Greatly in peace of thought; and have my fill

Of knowledge, what this vessel can contain;

Beyond which was my folly to aspire.   560

Henceforth I learn that to obey is best,

And love with fear the only God; to walk

As in his presence, ever to observe

---

559. this vessel. The human mind.

His providence, and on him sole depend,
Merciful over all his works, with good   565
Still overcoming evil, and by small
Accomplishing great things, by things deemed weak
Subverting worldly strong, and worldly wise
By simply meek; that suffering for truth's sake
Is fortitude to highest victory,   570
And to the faithful, death the gate of life;
Taught this by his example, whom I now
Acknowledge my redeemer ever blest.

   To whom thus also the angel last replied:
This having learned, thou hast attained the sum   575
Of wisdom; hope no higher, though all the stars
Thou knewst by name, and all the ethereal powers,
All secrets of the deep, all nature's works,
Or works of God in heaven, air, earth, or sea,
And all the riches of this world enjoyedst,   580
And all the rule, one empire; only add
Deeds to thy knowledge answerable; add faith,
Add virtue, patience, temperance; add love,
By name to come called charity, the soul
Of all the rest: then wilt thou not be loath   585
To leave this Paradise, but shalt possess
A paradise within thee, happier far.
Let us descend now therefore from this top
Of speculation; for the hour precise
Exacts our parting hence; and see the guards,   590

By me encamped on yonder hill, expect
Their motion, at whose front a flaming sword,
In signal of remove, waves fiercely round;
We may no longer stay; go, waken Eve;
Her also I with gentle dreams have calmed   595
Portending good, and all her spirits composed
To meek submission: thou at season fit
Let her with thee partake what thou hast heard,
Chiefly what may concern her faith to know,
The great deliverance by her seed to come   600
(For by the woman's seed) on all mankind,
That ye may live, which will be many days,
Both in one faith unanimous though sad,
With cause, for evils past, yet much more cheered
With meditation on the happy end.   605
    He ended, and they both descend the hill;
Descended, Adam to the bower where Eve
Lay sleeping ran before; but found her waked;
And thus with words not sad she him received.
    Whence thou returnst, and whither wentst, I know;   610
For God is also in sleep, and dreams advise,
Which he hath sent propitious, some great good
Presaging, since with sorrow and heart's distress
Wearied I fell asleep; but now lead on;
In me is no delay; with thee to go,   615
Is to stay here; without thee here to stay,
Is to go hence unwilling; thou to me

[221]

Art all things under heaven, all places thou,
Who for my wilful crime art banished hence.
This further consolation yet secure   620
I carry hence; though all by me is lost,
Such favour I unworthy am vouchsafed,
By me the promised seed shall all restore.
    So spake our mother Eve; and Adam heard
Well pleased, but answered not; for now too nigh   625
The archangel stood, and, from the other hill
To their fixed station, all in bright array
The cherubim descended; on the ground
Gliding meteorous, as evening mist
Ris'n from a river o'er the marish glides,   630
And gathers ground fast at the labourer's heel
Homeward returning. High in front advanced,
The brandished sword of God before them blazed,
Fierce as a comet; which with torrid heat,
And vapour as the Libyan air adust,   635
Began to parch that temperate clime; whereat
In either hand the hastening angel caught
Our lingering parents, and to the eastern gate
Led them direct, and down the cliff as fast
To the subjected plain; then disappeared.   640
They looking back, all the eastern side beheld

629. *Meteorous*. Like meteors.   630. *marish*. Marsh.   635. *adust*. Dried up.   640.
subjected. Lying below.

Of Paradise, so late their happy seat,
Waved over by that flaming brand; the gate
With dreadful faces thronged and fiery arms:
Some natural tears they dropped, but wiped them soon;   645
The world was all before them, where to choose
Their place of rest, and providence their guide:
They hand in hand with wandering steps and slow,
Through Eden took their solitary way.

AFTERWORD

Is *Paradise Lost* a Success?

At the start of the poem Milton asks his muse to help him 'justify the ways of God to men'. Few modern readers will feel that he succeeded in that aim. However, it could be argued that it was not Milton's fault. How an all-powerful, all-knowing God could have created a world that is full of suffering and evil has always been a problem for Christians, not only for Milton, and is so still. Since God is all-knowing, he must know, intimately and completely, about every occurrence of human suffering – every massacre, every tortured child, every lingering disease – before it happens, and since he is all-powerful he could have prevented it. To allow something to happen if you could have prevented it is to be responsible for it. So it follows that God is ultimately responsible for all suffering and all evil.

This is a fearsome conclusion, but Milton did not shrink from it. It is made clear in *Paradise Lost* that God foresees all the world's evil and yet allows it to happen.

It is true that Milton identifies two factors that might seem to lessen God's responsibility. The first is that, as God himself points out, he made man free (3:97–111). Since man fell of his own free will, it could be argued that the blame is man's, not God's.

If this point is examined a little more closely, though, it does not look so good for God. He made man free, he says, because otherwise he could have got no 'pleasure' from man's obedience (3:107). But God knew, when he created man, that he would be disobedient. It makes no sense to create a being whose obedience will give you pleasure if you know that that being is not going to be obedient.

The question that obviously arises is, could God have made man differently, and better? The answer must be yes, since God is all-powerful. He could have made man perfect. But he chose to make him imperfect, knowing that he would fall and incur the death penalty.

As if anticipating this objection, God protests that man 'had of me/All he could have' (3:98–9). If 'All he could have' means 'All I could give him', it is clearly untrue. God is almighty, so he could have created man exactly as he wished. He could have made him infallible, but chose not to.

If, on the other hand, 'All he could have' means 'All he could have, while still remaining within the limits of a human being', it is an empty claim, because God fixed what the limits of being a human being were, and, being almighty, could have widened them had he wished.

The second factor that seems to mitigate God's responsibility for evil is the redemption. It is built into God's plan that the Son will die to redeem mankind. However, the advantages of this arrangement should not be overstated. Christians in Milton's day, and for centuries before, agreed that the damned would far outnumber the saved. There was biblical evidence for this (Matt. 20:16, 'for many be called, but few chosen'), and it is endorsed in *Paradise Lost*, where the angel tells Adam that the 'far greater part' of mankind will fall away from the true faith (12:533).

So, despite the redemption, most humans will suffer in hell for all eternity, and God foresaw this before he created the human race. Even the devils are horrified, when they explore hell, by the ingenious array of supernatural ovens and refrigerators that God has prepared to torment the damned, who will be dragged, periodically, 'From beds of raging fire to starve in ice' (2:571–628).

Although modern readers are unlikely to find God's ways, as depicted in the poem, justified, from another viewpoint the cruel, angry, vengeful, praise-hungry God of *Paradise Lost*, who laughs at his helpless enemies, is one of the poem's successes. For this God, who seems morally repellent to us, was the true God, or so Milton believed. In the years prior to writing *Paradise Lost* he composed a long Latin work called *Christian Doctrine* in which he worked out, from the evidence of thousands of biblical quotations, what the biblical God was really like. Whether God was attractive was irrelevant. Milton was searching for the truth about God, pleasant or otherwise. He found, for example, that God punishes innocent children for their parents' sins, and he illustrates this practice, in *Christian Doctrine*, by referring to the treatment that women and children receive at the hands of conquering armies. That did not mean that he thought conquering armies attractive, only that he knew them to be factual.

Christian Doctrine would have been considered blasphemous at the time Milton wrote it. Publishing it was out of the question. So it was set aside, and remained undiscovered for almost two centuries. Instead, Milton put his morally repellent but biblically authentic God into *Paradise Lost*.

Another difficulty, and one that Milton successfully solves, is how to present the fall. In the Genesis account Adam and Eve's behaviour is inexplicable. They have been told that they will die if they eat the fruit, but Eve eats it because a talking snake tells her to, and she then gives it to Adam, who eats it without so much as a word of protest. It seems that God has entrusted the future of the human race to a couple who are not merely stupid but suicidal.

In Milton's rewritten account, however, their behaviour is psychologically believable and even, many readers have felt, justifiable. Eve's belief in her right to freedom and knowledge, which leads to her fall (9:745–79), echoes Milton's own firmly held opinions, as expressed, for example, in *Areopagitica*, his plea for the freedom of the press. Adam's decision to die with her has been widely praised as noble and heroic.

Even if we feel, though, that we should have behaved as they do, we can see that they sin, and that their sin consists of distrusting God. Eve trusts a snake rather than God; Adam cannot trust God to save Eve, so decides to die with her. What is required of a Christian, Milton believed, is unquestioning trust in God. That is what he expressed in the sonnet on his blindness, and Adam and Eve prove incapable of it. If we think we should have behaved as they do it only goes to show (Milton would have argued) that we are fallen beings.

It is true, of course, that unquestioning trust in the morally repellent God of *Paradise Lost* is a tough proposition. That is one of the factors that send tremors of dissent through the poem.

Is *Paradise Lost* a Christian Poem?

Milton certainly considered himself a Christian. But one distinguishing feature of Christian belief is absent from his poetry. That feature is the crucifixion. In the crucifixion God becomes a man, makes himself helpless, and allows himself to be tormented and nailed to a cross. As he dies in agony, he prays to his Father to forgive his killers. None of the old religions came near to imagining such an event. It was new because it gave a new meaning to the idea of triumph. The Christian God triumphs by allowing himself to be defeated. His strength is to make himself helpless.

The other Christian poets of the seventeenth century contemplate the crucifixion with awe and pity. Milton is the exception. It seems that he was unwilling to imagine the physical agonies of the dying Saviour. In *Paradise Lost* the crucifixion is allocated a single line (12:413). Milton had tried to write a poem on the subject when he was in his twenties. It was called *The Passion*, and he managed some fifty lines of frigid bombast before he gave up, saying that he was 'nothing satisfied' with it.

The psychological and cultural reasons for Milton's avoidance can only be guessed at. One may have been the popularity of the crucifixion as a subject in Catholic counter-Reformation art. But the exclusion of the crucifixion from his writing may also reflect how deeply he was influenced – and damaged – by the example of Greek and Roman literature. His models for heroic poetry were Homer's *Iliad* and Virgil's *Aeneid*, and both these epics adhered to the classical concept of triumph, which means defeating and killing an enemy in battle. As a poet, Milton seems to have retained this as the natural way to imagine triumph, and it is the mode in which both Satan and God pursue their antagonism.

Some moments in *Paradise Lost* point towards an alternative, Christian kind of triumph, but they are few and brief. In the introduction to Book 9 Milton rejects classical poetry's glorification of triumph in battle, and complains that 'the better fortitude/ Of patience and heroic martyrdom' has been neglected by poets (9:31–2). Yet he neglects it himself. The war in heaven is an old-style battle-piece, and the fallen angels are ejected from heaven by a prodigious display of military power, not by patience and martyrdom.

Adam, in his closing speech, says that he is 'greatly instructed' by what he has learned in the course of the poem about how God proceeds: 'By things deemed weak/Subverting worldly strong, and worldly wise/By simply meek' (12:567–9). But it is hard to see how Adam can have gathered, from the events of the poem, that the God of *Paradise Lost* operates in this way, or that weakness and meekness are in his line at all.

There is only one speaker in the poem who thinks deeply enough to point out the futility of violence as a means of settling disputes, and that speaker is Satan, who remarks crisply: 'Who overcomes/By force, hath overcome but half his foe' (1:648–9).

In its unwillingness to contemplate the crucifixion, then, and in its adherence to the old ideal of triumphant militarism, *Paradise Lost* is not a Christian poem.

Another aspect of Christianity that readers of *Paradise Lost* might expect to find, but do not, is belief in a loving God. The reason for this may be traced to Milton's theology. He was heretical, by seventeenth-century standards, in that he did not believe in the Holy Trinity. In his theology, worked out in *Christian Doctrine*, the Father and the Son are separate beings, and the Son is subordinate. The Son has not existed from all eternity, as the Father has, and the Son owes all his powers to the Father. He is merely a receptacle for whatever abilities his Father chooses to bestow on him.

Paradise Lost reflects these beliefs, in that the Father and the Son are separate and have different characters. The Son's face shows 'Love without end' (3:142). But the Father seems more concerned with anger and justice than with love. When the Father asks for a volunteer to die for mankind – 'Say, heavenly powers, where shall we find such love?' (3:213) – the implication is that the extreme of self-sacrificing love that is required is an attribute of the Son rather than of the Father. Christian readers expecting an eternal God to die for mankind will look in vain for such a figure in Milton's poem.

Further, even though the Son's face is said to show 'Love without end', he never says anything that convinces us he loves mankind as, say, Adam loves Eve. What the Son mostly expresses is obsequiousness towards and congratulation of his Father. Even when he volunteers to die for mankind the level of discourse is that of a legal agreement. If the Son – just once – burst out with an expression of his love of mankind when he saw how beautiful humans were, as Satan does, it would transform the whole poem. But he never does.

FURTHER READING

Though neglected by the general reader, Milton is tirelessly quarried by academics. Books and articles, in print and online, pour out of British and American universities each year. What follows is a brief, personal selection.

Editions of Milton's Poetry

Paradise Lost, ed. Alastair Fowler, Longman, second edition, 1998.
Complete Shorter Poems, ed. John Carey, Longman, second edition, 1997.
Originally published together, these two volumes provide, for every poem Milton wrote, extensive explanatory notes and summaries of relevant criticism and scholarship.

Milton's Life and Personality

Gordon Campbell and Thomas N. Corns, *John Milton: Life, Work, and Thought*, Oxford University Press, 2008. The most authoritative and up-to-date biography.
Colin Burrow, 'Shall I Go On?', *London Review of Books*, no. 5, 7 March 2013. So far as I know, this is the best – and funniest – attempt by a leading scholar to capture Milton's personality.

The Reception of *Paradise Lost*

John Leonard, *Faithful Labourers: A Reception History of Paradise Lost, 1667–1970*, Oxford University Press, 2013. A hugely erudite, two-volume compendium.

Criticism and Comment

The mid-twentieth-century Milton controversy began with attacks on Milton as poet by T. S. Eliot and the Cambridge critic F. R. Leavis, and developed into disagreements about the God of *Paradise Lost*, with C. S. Lewis and William Empson as the chief protagonists. Landmark publications (in chronological order) were:

F. R. Leavis, 'Milton's Verse', in *Revaluation: Tradition and Development in English Poetry*, Chatto & Windus, 1936.

T. S. Eliot, 'A Note on the Verse of John Milton', in *Essays and Studies of the English Association*, Clarendon Press, 1936.

C. S. Lewis, *A Preface to Paradise Lost*, Oxford University Press, 1942.

A. J. A. Waldock, *Paradise Lost and Its Critics*, Cambridge University Press, 1947.

John Peter, *A Critique of Paradise Lost*, Columbia University Press, 1960.

William Empson, *Milton's God*, New Directions, 1961.

Christopher Ricks, *Milton's Grand Style*, Oxford University Press, 1963.

Dennis H. Burden, *The Logical Epic*, Routledge & Kegan Paul, 1967.

Some notable examples, mostly of more recent criticism, are:

Catherine Belsey, *John Milton: Language, Gender, Power*, Oxford University Press, 1988.

Dennis R. Danielson, *Milton's Good God*, Cambridge University Press, 1982.

J. Martin Evans, *Paradise Lost and the Genesis Tradition*, Oxford University Press, 1968.

Stanley Fish, *Surprised by Sin*, University of California Press, 1967.

Maggie Kilgour, *Milton and the Metamorphosis of Ovid*, Oxford University Press, 2012.

Christopher Hill, *Milton and the English Revolution*, Faber & Faber, 1977.

John Leonard, *Naming in Paradise: Milton and the Language of Adam and Eve*, Oxford University Press, 1990.

Neil Forsyth, *The Satanic Epic*, Princeton University Press, 2003.

Diane Kelsey McColley, *Milton's Eve*, University of Illinois Press, 1983.

William Poole, *Milton and the Idea of the Fall*, Cambridge University Press, 2005.

David Quint, *Inside Paradise Lost. Reading the Design of Milton's Epic*, Princeton University Press, 2014.

Louis Schwartz, *Milton and Maternal Mortality*, Cambridge University Press, 2009.